The publisher gratefully acknowledges the generous support of the Classical Literature Endowment Fund of the University of California Press Foundation, which was established by a major gift from Joan Palevsky.

Caligula

Bust of Caligula. Copenhagen, Ny Carlsberg Glyptotek 637 (Inv. 1453).
Photo: Ole Haupt.

Caligula

A Biography

Aloys Winterling

Translated by Deborah Lucas Schneider,
Glenn W. Most, and Paul Psoinos

UNIVERSITY OF CALIFORNIA PRESS

Berkeley   Los Angeles   London

University of California Press, one of the most distinguished university presses in the United States, enriches lives around the world by advancing scholarship in the humanities, social sciences, and natural sciences. Its activities are supported by the UC Press Foundation and by philanthropic contributions from individuals and institutions. For more information, visit www.ucpress.edu.

University of California Press
Berkeley and Los Angeles, California

University of California Press, Ltd.
London, England

Library of Congress Cataloging-in-Publication Data

Winterling, Aloys.
    [Caligula. English]
    Caligula : a biography / Aloys Winterling ; translated by Deborah
Lucas Schneider, Glenn W. Most, and Paul Psoinos
        p.   cm.
    Originally published in German: München : C.H. Beck, c2003,
with title Caligula : eine Biographie.
    Includes bibliographical references and index.
    ISBN 978-0-520-24895-3 (cloth, alk. paper)
    1. Caligula, Emperor of Rome, 12–41.   2. Rome—History—Caligula, 37–41.
3. Emperors—Rome—Biography.   I. Title.

DG283.W5613   2011
937'.07092—dc22   2011012924

Manufactured in the United States of America

20 19 18 17 16 15 14 13 12 11
10 9 8 7 6 5 4 3 2 1

CONTENTS

Conclusion: Inventing the Mad Emperor
187

ABBREVIATIONS

Dig.	*Digesta Justiniani*
Dio	Cassius Dio, *Roman History*
Jos. *Ant.*	Flavius Josephus, *Antiquitates Judaicae*
Phil. *Leg.*	Philo, *Legatio ad Gaium*
Sen. *Ad Helv.*	Seneca, *Ad Helviam Matrem de Consolatione*
De Const. Sap.	Seneca, *De Constantia Sapientis*
Suet. *Aug.*	Suetonius, *De Vita Caesarum libri: Augustus*
Cal.	Suetonius, *De Vita Caesarum libri:* *Gaius Caligula*
Claud.	Suetonius, *De Vita Caesarum libri: Claudius*
Tib.	Suetonius, *De Vita Caesarum libri: Tiberius*
Vit.	Suetonius, *De Vita Caesarum libri: Vitellius*
Tac. *Ann.*	Tacitus, *Annales*

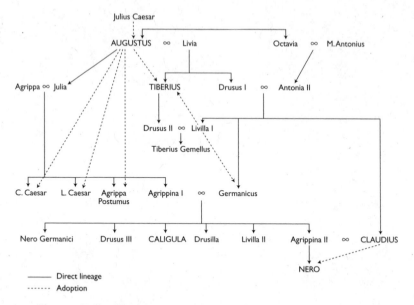

Figure 1. Ruling Emperors.

A Mad Emperor?

Caligula, the man who was Roman emperor from A.D. 37 to 41, started out as a tyrannical ruler and degenerated into a monster. He drank pearls dissolved in vinegar and ate food covered with gold leaf. He forced men and women of high rank to have sex with him, turned part of his palace into a brothel, and even committed incest with his own sisters. The chief victims of his senseless cruelty were Roman senators. Torture and executions were the order of the day. He removed two consuls from office because they had forgotten his birthday. He considered himself superhuman and forced contemporaries to worship him as a god. He wanted to make his horse a consul and planned to move the capital of the Empire from Rome to Alexandria.

His biographer Suetonius, to whom we owe most of this information, and the other ancient sources have an explanation for this behavior: He was insane. The philosopher Seneca, a contemporary who knew him personally, mentions his "madness" and calls him a "beast." Another contemporary, Philo of Alexandria, who had contact with him as the head of a legation, speaks of his "insanity." Pliny the Elder and Flavius Josephus, two authors writing several decades later, mention his absurd behavior and report on his "madness." At the beginning of the second century Tacitus, the most noted historian of the Roman Empire, whose account of Caligula's reign has been lost, speaks of the emperor's "troubled brain." Suetonius, who wrote his biography a little less than a hundred years after Caligula's death, considered him to have been "mentally ill," and Cassius Dio, who wrote a voluminous history of Rome at the start of the third century, also believed that the emperor had "lost his head."

No wonder, then, that modern scholarship has followed these conclusions: "Imperial madness" is the standard explanation. Ludwig Quidde, who made this term famous at the end of the nineteenth century, describes this "disease" as "megalomania, carried to the point of regarding oneself as divine; disregard for all limits of law and all the rights of other individuals; brutal cruelty without purpose or reason." Although these elements are also found "in other mentally ill people," the unique quality of an emperor's madness lay in his position as ruler, which "provides particularly fertile soil for the seeds of such a predisposition and permits them to develop unhindered in a manner that is otherwise hardly possible." For Quidde's contemporaries, however, this brief biographical sketch of Caligula had a double meaning, a hidden intention beneath the surface of the words. They saw the depiction as so clearly aimed simultaneously at another emperor, Kaiser Wilhelm II of Germany—who was certainly not insane—that Quidde's book ran through thirty printings within a short time. It also earned the author three months in prison and ended his academic career. Yet these events did not weaken the impact of his conclusions about Caligula. The author of a recent biography (published in 1991) still describes the emperor as "crazy," and a recent survey of the scholarly literature contains references to his "imperial madness."

Readers of this biography of Caligula thus appear to be in for quite a story—and indeed they are. Matters are considerably more complicated than might appear at first glance, however. It was established during the nineteenth century that ancient accounts of this emperor are by no means as much in agreement as they may seem. Take Caligula's sex life, for example: The claim that the emperor committed incest with his three sisters is misinformation that surfaces for the first time in Suetonius. Its hollowness is easily proved: The emperor's two contemporaries Seneca and Philo, who were both familiar with aristocratic circles in Rome and well informed, heap invective on the emperor and would hardly have failed to mention such a charge had it been in circulation then. But clearly they knew nothing about it. The same holds for Tacitus. In his history of the early Empire he discusses at some length the dissolute life of the younger Agrippina, who was Caligula's sister and the wife of the later emperor Claudius. He even considers her capable of having attempted incest with her own son, the emperor Nero. Clearly he would have mentioned any incest between Agrippina and her brother, which would have suited his account, but no such allegation was known to him. Thus the story was invented at some point after Caligula's death.

A further example: A broadly based conspiracy against Caligula took place midway through the year 39, in which many members of the Roman aristocracy participated, including an important military commander in Germania, the emperor's sisters, his closest confidant among the senators, and the sitting consuls. It was a highly dramatic occurrence, which threatened the emperor's life and fundamentally altered his behavior toward his fellow members of the senatorial order. Curiously, the early sources are completely silent on the matter. Suetonius does not devote a single word to the conspiracy itself; he describes only the emperor's apparently confused reactions to it. Yet two casual references to it in his biographies of the emperors Claudius and Vespasian reveal that the events, which are also documented in inscriptions, were well known to him.

Many more examples could easily be given, as will become apparent later. They point to the following conclusion: The accounts of Caligula surviving from antiquity pursue the clearly recognizable goal of depicting the emperor as an irrational monster. They provide demonstrably false information to support this picture of him and omit information that could contradict it. They present the emperor's actions out of context, so that their original significance is either completely obscured or can be grasped only with great difficulty. The authors offer assessments of his behavior that often contradict other information contained in their very own accounts.

And finally on the matter of his insanity: Ancient scholars discussed the phenomena and causes of psychopathology from the fifth century B.C. on. During the reign of the emperor Tiberius, Caligula's predecessor, the Roman author Cornelius Celsus wrote on this subject in his books on medicine (*De Medicina*). Celsus characterizes insanity (*insania*) as a disease that manifests itself in senseless behavior or incomprehensible speech. He describes two categories of patients: those who have delusions but whose intellectual reasoning is otherwise unimpaired, and those whose reason is itself disturbed. Later medical authors who employ the same distinction give as an example of the former a man named Theophilus, who—although he could speak and reason properly otherwise—believed that he was constantly surrounded by people playing flutes, making noises, and observing him. He often upset the household by shouting orders that these interlopers should be thrown out. As an example of the latter ailment the authors describe a patient who suffered from the delusion that he had no head. He believed that he was a beheaded tyrant.

The subject was covered in Roman law as well. A series of texts on homicide, treason (*maiestas*), libel, and property damage declare that "the insane" (*furiosi, insani*) are not legally responsible for their actions. "What delinquency...can there be in a person who is not in his right mind?" asks the legal scholar Pegasus (*Dig.* 9.2.5.2).* It is even noted specifically that in the case of crimes committed by someone of unsound mind, it is not the perpetrator himself who deserves punishment, but rather those who failed to keep watch over him.

How should we imagine the situation in the case of Caligula? Do we suppose that there is a Roman emperor who behaves irrationally, whose speech is incomprehensible, whose perceptions of reality are disturbed, and who commits all sorts of crimes in this condition, without anyone's intervening to stop him? If that had been so then an accusation of insanity would have had to be leveled, not at the emperor, but rather at the society that surrounded him: at the Roman aristocracy first and foremost, meaning the Senate that carried out his decisions, the magistrates in Rome who followed his instructions, and the military commanders and governors in the Empire who obeyed his orders. Blame would

---

* Citations from ancient sources are based on the translations in the Loeb Classical Library; the full forms for the abbreviations used for authors' names and works are listed on page vii.

fall also upon the treasury officials who reallocated enormous sums at his behest, upon the people who saw him daily and advised him, and lastly upon the people of Rome themselves, who cheered him at the Circus and theater. If Caligula was mad, why wasn't he silently removed from public view and placed under the care of a physician—just as was done when rulers in later European history became mentally ill?

By no means do all modern authors assume Caligula was insane. In view of the clearly denunciatory tendency of the ancient sources, a number of scholars—notably Willrich, Gelzer, Balsdon, and Barrett—have attempted to clarify what actually occurred under his rule. Great progress has been made on some particular questions: By comparing contemporaneous sources and earlier traditions with later ones, it has been possible to weed out false information, like the allegation of incest. Assertions by ancient authors that contradict the intention of their own works—statements that have crept in by mistake, as it were, or references to events too well known to be omitted—have been shown to be reliable. And finally scholars can draw on the entire body of surviving documents to become familiar with the broader context of the times and develop a theory of the politics, society, religion, and mindsets of the period; this makes it possible to distinguish between plausible and implausible reports in the sources. To some extent modern scholarship has gone too far in transforming a ruler depicted as immoral and insane into a good one whose actions were rational. Above all, however, one question remains open: How can one explain the intense hatred for Caligula that is expressed in ancient accounts of him?

Almost all the sources can be traced back to members of the Roman aristocracy. They stem from senators and knights who were in direct contact with the emperor. Thus even their false statements about Caligula contain a degree of historical truth: The Roman aristocracy must have experienced such appalling things under his rule that posthumously he was tarred with the worst possible stigma: He was reviled as a monster and a madman and thus expelled outright from human society.

ONE

Childhood and Youth

THE LEGACY OF AUGUSTUS

Gaius Caesar Germanicus was born on 31 August in the year A.D. 12 to Germanicus and the elder Agrippina. At the time no one could have foreseen that at the age of only twenty-four this young man, known by then under his nickname, "Caligula," would become Roman emperor. On 18 March 37, he would become ruler of an empire that spanned virtually the entire known world of antiquity, from Syria to the English Channel, from North Africa to the Danube region, and from Spain to Asia Minor. No one could have anticipated how many intrigues and murders, trials and executions would take place in Rome, the center of that Empire, in the two and a half decades leading up to his succession. Nor could anyone have possibly imagined in the year 12 how Gaius would come to exercise his rule in the end.

At the time of his birth, his great-grandfather Augustus was still in power. Although aristocrats criticized Augustus in private, they were all agreed on the most important achievement of

Figure 2. Bust of Caligula. Heraklion, Archaeological Museum, 64.

his long sole rule (31 B.C.–A.D. 14): After almost a hundred years of violent political conflict and civil wars, which had affected the entire Mediterranean region and could be described in retrospect as a process of gathering monopolization of political power, Augustus had brought peace. Admittedly in doing so he had also ended the old collective rule of the aristocracy that had characterized the Roman Republic and functioned with great success for centuries, replacing it with a form of sole rule—something that had clearly become unavoidable. His exceptional position, which he had usurped during the civil war against Marcus Antonius, was based on military might, but he had not given it the form of monarchy, showing a restraint for which many of his senatorial coequals gave him credit. Instead he had chosen the term "principate," which allowed him to appear as merely one of the first among citizens. At the same time he had reanimated the old political institutions and practices of the Republic: The Senate met and debated; the magistrates in Rome and the provincial governors performed their tasks; the people assembled, voted, and decided—and acted on important questions only as Augustus wished. The emperor's unrestricted control over the military was symbolized by his bodyguard, the elite Praetorians, whose presence and its import could not be overlooked. Nevertheless he had caused his unique position to be confirmed in Rome and the provinces in the traditional legal forms, showing that although he had drained the old Republican institutions of real power he still needed them to justify his authority. Thus a curious situation had arisen, one that demanded great communicative skill from all participants: The senators had to act as if they still possessed a degree of power that they no longer had, while the emperor had to exercise his power in such a way as to dissemble his possession of it.

How did this contradictory, historically unique combination of republic and monarchy come about? One social and one political reason can be named. Like all highly developed pre-modern cultures, ancient Rome had a stratified society, with a deep division between the nobility and the non-noble population. The exercise of authority, whether in the military or in the civic sphere, had always been limited to members of the upper class. Even though the common people were included in the political process during the Republic, it was precisely their behavior that reserved authority for the noble families. For although elections were held regularly and were technically open to non-noble candidates, again and again those elected to political office (and thus to positions of military leadership) came almost exclusively from the same noble families. They were evidently the only men whom the common people were prepared to obey. Every emperor faced this situation. He needed the leading members of the nobility to command the Roman legions throughout the Empire and to perform civic functions in Rome itself. This group was identical, however, to the approximately six hundred men who composed the membership of the Senate—the most important Republican political institution—and the core of the Roman aristocracy, with whom an emperor thus had to have some kind of workable entente.

A second reason for the situation was more banal, but just as important. It involved the mortal danger to which all participants were exposed. The civil wars of the late Republic had shown what ruthlessness military leaders were capable of in dealing with their fellow aristocrats. Since the time of Sulla there had been repeated proscriptions in which political and personal opponents had simply been liquidated. Conversely, however, it had become apparent that in Rome bayonets did not make a good throne, so to speak. The fate of the all-powerful dictator Caesar, the adoptive father of Augustus, had shown that the aristocratic Roman resistance to all forms of monarchy could stiffen into assassination, even within the circle of the ruler's most trusted followers. Conspiracy and murder, ever justifiable for removing tyrants, became swords of Damocles hanging over the head of every emperor from then on. As the coming centuries were to show, more than a few would fall victim to them.

Augustus's answer to this situation was the paradoxical establishment of sole rule through restoration of the old Republic. His particular achievement consisted in demonstrating that such a thing was possible. Augustus's precedent, however, proved exceedingly difficult to follow. Attempts to reproduce it became the dominant feature of the period after his death in the year 14, and thus also of the world in which his great-grandson Caligula came of age. Two central problems above all rapidly became apparent: the personal inadequacy of possible successors for the difficult role of emperor, and the complicating politicization of the imperial family (a process that could be observed even during Augustus's lifetime).

Augustus's style of ruling demanded both a high degree of dissimulation regarding his own position and great skill in handling power. For several centuries a social system had been established based on an immediate link between political power and social status. The members of the aristocracy, whose goal in life—as in other pre-modern aristocratic societies—was to acquire honor and fame, depended for that purpose on exercising political functions and holding office as magistrates. Success in these endeavors determined an individual's ranking in the social hierarchy of the aristocracy, and this status was visible in many aspects of everyday life: in the order in which senators voted; in seating at theatrical performances in Rome; in the number of followers who paid morning calls at the home of a successful aristocratic politician and accompanied him to the Forum; in the location and size of his house, and in the luxury displayed there, especially at dinners and banquets.

One condition of Augustus's success was his willingness, in social situations, to dispense with displays of the political power he had acquired. In daily life he behaved like an ordinary senator, maintaining friendships with other aristocrats as if they were equals, refraining from appearing in public with a large retinue, and residing in a house on the Palatine Hill that was reported to be relatively modest by aristocratic standards. Via this renunciation of honors Augustus was evidently following a conscious strategy, to ensure that the aristocracy accepted his position. In so doing he overcame the typical aristocratic mentality, and he was successful primarily because his contemporaries retained their traditional outlook. This was an extraordinary achievement on his part and, as the subsequent history would show, one that few of his successors were willing or able to emulate.

Augustus's willingness to forgo special honors was connected with a style of ruling that dispensed entirely with giving orders to members of the Senate, but nevertheless offered sufficient clues for them to grasp what his wishes were. Because of his superior position of power the senators automatically obeyed his intimations, in a thoroughly opportunistic manner that sometimes even anticipated any actual hint or sign. Yet it was decisive that traditional forms were observed. Thus it was sufficient for the emperor to break off his personal friendship with a recalcitrant senator and deny him admittance to his house. Immediately other senators would see to it that he was charged with a crime and brought to trial; as a result the careers of the emperor's "enemies" soon came to an end, and often their lives as well. The art in Augustus's dealings with the aristocracy consisted in making such serious cases the rare exception, even though a whole series of conspiracies against him were discovered and exposed.

Augustus implemented wise policies on particular issues, such as increasing the security of the Empire and its infrastructure, adding architectural adornments to Rome, or keeping its citizens supplied with grain. But fundamentally his grip on success came not from policy, but from his personal ability to master paradoxical demands in communicating with the aristocracy: ruling without giving orders, wielding power without appearing to do so. At the end of his life, it is reported, he sent for the members of his inner circle, delivered a cynical commentary on the times, and asked for a round of applause, like a star retiring from the stage. His immediate successor would demonstrate that such acting skills were rare among the Roman aristocracy.

THE POLITICAL FAMILY

Because Augustus had not introduced a monarchy in a constitutional sense, arranging instead for the institutions of the Republic to grant him special powers tailored to his own needs, it was an open question who would legally succeed him. The characteristic motto of hereditary monarchies—"The king is dead; long live the king!"—did not apply to the Roman Empire. In Theodor Mommsen's classic phrase, "by law the Principate died with the *princeps*." Every time an emperor died, someone had to emerge as the next wielder of supreme power, to be proclaimed emperor by the army, and to be confirmed by the Senate. In the worst-case scenario—as it played out after Nero's death in the year 68 or that of Commodus in 192—that meant the outbreak of a new civil war, until one of the claimants emerged as victor. Normally an emperor would make arrangements for the succession during his lifetime. It was crucial, however, that in principle he had a free hand to choose a successor. To start with, the identity of the next emperor was an open question.

Usually it was not only the family fortune that was passed on from father to son in aristocratic families in ancient Rome; sons also inherited the close relationships within the aristocratic society, alliances known as "friendships," as well as any political prestige that the father had enjoyed with the people of Rome and the soldiers of the Empire. If the emperor had a son or had adopted one, that son was thus automatically destined to be the successor. Women, especially wives or daughters of an emperor, could also play a crucial role in the question of succession if they had a son from a previous marriage or had given birth to a grandson of the emperor. As a result family relationships acquired great political significance, which could destabilize the position of a reigning emperor as well as support it.

Although Augustus had no son of his own, he did have a daughter, Julia, from a former marriage. His second wife, Livia, for her part had brought two sons with her into the marriage: Tiberius, the later emperor, and Drusus (known as Drusus I, or Drusus the Elder). Augustus chose to signal and secure his choice by arranging for the presumptive successor to marry Julia: first his nephew Marcellus and then, after Marcellus's early demise, his chief general and associate, Marcus Agrippa. When Agrippa also died in 12 B.C. Augustus adopted his two grandsons from Julia and Agrippa's marriage, Gaius and Lucius, who thus became candidates for the throne. Both of them also predeceased Augustus, however, so that the choice finally fell on his stepson Tiberius. He, too, had to marry Julia, and of all the candidates was the one who actually lived to become her father's successor.

The politics of the imperial family had, however, produced other aspirants for the throne. Augustus had married off his second stepson, Drusus, to his niece, Antonia II (Antonia Minor, Antonia the Younger). At the time of Drusus's death in 9 B.C. they had two sons—Claudius, the later emperor, and Germanicus—who were thus great-nephews of the emperor. Claudius received little notice initially because of a physical handicap, but for Germanicus a marriage was arranged with Agrippina the Elder, Augustus's granddaughter from the marriage of Julia and Agrippa. Germanicus and Agrippina's children included three sons: Nero (not the later emperor), another Drusus (III), and Caligula. At the time of Augustus's death they were all still children, but unlike Tiberius they acquired the prestige of the imperial family by virtue of being the first emperor's biological great-grandchildren and great-great-nephews. Augustus "solved" this problem by requiring Tiberius to adopt Germanicus, thereby opening the way to the succession for his great-grandchildren. The fate of Tiberius's own son, Drusus II (Drusus the Younger) remained undecided. An attempt was made to resolve it by arranging further marriages between the different branches of the imperial family. Thus Drusus the Younger married Livilla, Augustus's great-niece, while Livilla's daughter in her turn married one of Germanicus's sons, Nero. One last grandson of Augustus, named Agrippa Postumus, from the marriage of Julia and Agrippa, had fallen into disfavor for reasons that remain unclear. He was murdered in the year 14, possibly on Augustus's own initiative or that of Livia or Tiberius.

These complicated family relationships—difficult not only for modern prosopographers, but probably also for contemporaries to keep straight—signal a central problem that resulted directly from Augustus's construction of the Principate. Because he chose to forgo a hereditary monarchy and thus the concomitant legal clarification of the succession, he found it difficult to control the political prestige derived from blood relationships to the emperor. Rivalries could arise within the imperial family, which in turn offered ideal openings for groups of aristocrats to back possible successors. Sometimes these alliances developed into conspiracies. Augustus's own daughter, Julia, started the ball rolling. In the year 2 B.C. she was banished because of her contacts with young aristocrats in Rome, including Iullus Antonius, the son of the triumvir Marcus Antonius, who had been Augustus's last remaining rival in the civil war. Whether adultery was involved, as the official charge claimed, or a political conspiracy, as many suspected, is in the last analysis irrelevant. If the daughter of the emperor, whose three marriages had created presumptive candidates to succeed him, entered into a close relationship with a high-ranking aristocrat, that in itself amounted to an important political development that threatened the emperor, regardless of what her own motives may have been.

Similar events would occur repeatedly over the decades that followed. All these conspiracies, real or imagined, and the punitive reactions to them meant that when the emperor Nero died in the year 68, not a single descendant of Augustus remained alive. This complete disappearance of the imperial family can hardly be judged in moral terms. It resulted from the political relevance of those familial relationships and the potential mortal danger menacing all the emperor's kin.

A CHILDHOOD AS "LITTLE BOOTS"

Caligula spent his first seven years in Germania, Rome, Greece, and the Orient. As many sources attest, his father, Germanicus, who had risen to the status of prince through Augustus's adoption arrangements, enjoyed great popularity in all parts of society on account of his good looks and genial personality; he was made commander of the Roman legions on the Rhine in the year 13. His task there was to lead a campaign against the Germanic tribes east of the river, who had inflicted a major defeat on the Romans in the Teutoburg Forest a few years earlier. Germanicus's wife, Agrippina, followed him, and soon afterwards their small son was sent north to join them, too. He thus spent his early years in a military camp. Supposedly it was Agrippina, known to take an active interest in military affairs, who hit on the idea of dressing little Gaius in a kind of miniature legionary's uniform, as a form of flattery to the soldiers and designed to win their affection. He acquired his nickname, "Caligula," from the little soldier's boots he wore, and it stuck to him for his entire life.

Agrippina had anticipated the soldiers' reaction correctly. The little boy became the favorite of the legions' camp. After the death of Augustus, when the armies of the Rhine mounted a dangerous mutiny and tried to proclaim Germanicus emperor even against his will, the child is thought to have played a decisive role. When the precarious situation prompted the commander to send his wife and child to safety in Trier with their retinue, the solders are supposed to have become ashamed and called off the uprising. According to another source they took Caligula hostage to prevent his removal from the camp.

In early summer of the year 17 the family returned to Rome, where Germanicus was honored with a triumph for his campaigns against the Germanic tribes. Such a procession to celebrate a commander's victories was the traditional apex of an aristocrat's career, and a huge enhancement to his family's prestige, but a goal achieved by very few. Germanicus's triumph is said to have been staged with exceptional pomp. Trophies, prisoners, and depictions of the mountains, rivers, and battlefields were included, so that the Roman public could get a vivid picture of the popular general's feats. Caligula, not quite five years old, and his four siblings stood at the center of the grand display with which the city celebrated Rome's military success in the North and honored Germanicus: "To the spectators the effect was heightened by the noble figure of the commander himself," writes Tacitus in his *Annals,* "and by the five children who loaded his chariot" (2.41.3).

The stay in Rome lasted only a few months. Already in the fall of the same year Germanicus was given the task of reorganizing governmental affairs in the eastern part of the Empire. Again his wife, Agrippina, accompanied him, and so did Caligula, while the other children remained behind in Rome. The trip turned out to be a combination of educational journey and ruler's progress. In addition to his military skills Germanicus is reported to have been very knowledgeable about Greek and Roman traditions and well versed in literature; he is thought to have written comic plays in Greek himself. The group visited the site of the naval battle at Actium, where Augustus (then still known as Octavian) had defeated Marcus Antonius, Germanicus's grandfather. The next stop was Athens, followed by the islands of Euboea and then Lesbos, where Agrippina gave birth to another child, Livilla. They then traveled through northwestern

Asia Minor to Byzantium and the Black Sea before returning to the Aegean coast. After making an excursion to Troy the family headed for Syria next, making intermediate stops that included Rhodes. Everywhere the potential successor to the throne, his wife, and their small son were received with great honor. As we know from surviving inscriptions and coins, several cities used the opportunity to commemorate Germanicus and Agrippina as deities, a form of honoring rulers that had a long tradition in the Greek East. Twenty years later the town of Assos on the coast of Asia Minor reminded Caligula, then emperor, that he had first set foot on the soil of the province of Asia there in the company of his father.

From Syria the group proceeded to a further country under Roman influence: Armenia, where a new king was crowned. After seeing to the reorganization of some parts of the Roman administration, particularly in Cappadocia and Commagene, Germanicus proceeded with his family to the famous ancient city of Alexandria. It was here that the Ptolemaic kings had resided in their magnificent palaces, but also where Caesar and Antonius had lived with Queen Cleopatra. The inhabitants of the city, which had served as an opposite pole to Rome during the civil war, staged great festivities to celebrate Germanicus's arrival. After an excursion up the Nile to see Memphis and the Pyramids, the family returned to Syria.

There the journey came to a sudden and tragic end. Germanicus fell ill and died on 10 October of the year 19, at the age of thirty-three. An open quarrel had broken out with Gnaeus Calpurnius Piso, the governor of Syria, and as he lay dying Germanicus accused the governor of poisoning him. A rumor to this effect quickly spread and soon acquired the added detail that the actual instigator had been the emperor Tiberius himself. It was said he had plotted the murder of his adopted son because Germanicus's great popularity with the common people and soldiers had turned him into a rival.

On his father's death Caligula, then a boy of seven, was thrust into the spotlight for the last time during his childhood. He was once again at the center of extraordinary events, but now of a sad kind. When Agrippina, accompanied by Caligula and Livilla, arrived in Brindisi with the urn containing her husband's ashes, she was met by a huge crowd of mourners. Two cohorts of the Praetorian Guard provided an escort for the family's onward journey. Drusus, the son of Tiberius, and Claudius, Germanicus's brother, came as far as the town of Tarracina to meet them, accompanied by the four other children, the consuls, the Senate, and citizens from the city. They escorted the procession back to Rome, where Germanicus's remains were interred in the Mausoleum of Augustus. Vast crowds of Romans lined the streets for his funeral.

For Caligula, his father's death was a major turning point in his life in more respects than one, for it affected not only his family. He had spent his first seven years in an elevated position in a milieu dominated entirely by monarchic institutions. The role played by a Roman general in war was monarchical, and the position of a Roman governor in the provinces resembled that of a monarch. At the legionaries' camp on the Rhine, in the triumph at Rome, and on the journey through the eastern parts of the Empire, Caligula had always been presented to a public that transferred some of its veneration for the outstanding prince Germanicus to his small son. The general popularity that "Little Boots" thus enjoyed became visible again eighteen years later in the enthusiasm with which the population greeted his accession to the throne. In the intervening years, however, Caligula would have very different experiences. The admiration showered on him when he stood beside a future emperor gave way to a long phase marked by peril and mortal enmities. Along with the rest of his family Caligula was exposed to such threats, which cost his mother and brothers their lives.

CONDITIONS IN ANCIENT ROME UNDER TIBERIUS

The reign of Tiberius (14–37) was of central importance not only to young Caligula personally, but also to the development of the emperor's position, which had implications for Caligula's own later rule. Difficult as it is to sum up the character and actions of the second Roman emperor, one conclusion is irrefutable: The legacy left him by his stepfather and adoptive father, Augustus, required the emperor to play a complex role, and Tiberius never grew into it. One could say that while Augustus did play the part like a consummate actor, Tiberius took it all at face value. If the former *princeps* had exercised his power vis-à-vis the aristocracy by pretending that he did not possess it, then the latter had the power but did not exercise it. And if during the rule of Augustus the senators could pretend that they were exercising power that they did not possess, under Tiberius they possessed power that they could not exercise.

The new emperor's first step had been to make sure he controlled the armed forces; the Praetorian Guard and the legions had to swear an oath of allegiance to him. From time to time he summoned the guard to drill in front of the assembled senators as a visible demonstration of his power. He disapproved, however, of the evident result of this situation, already discernible under Augustus—namely that the members of the aristocracy, whose chances for advancement depended to a great extent on the emperor's favor, attempted to guess what he wanted and then behaved opportunistically to gratify him. Tiberius acted as if the Republic had been restored in actual fact. He frequently had the Senate debate matters related to the real exercise of power without letting the senators know his own position, but was then highly displeased when they reached decisions counter to his wishes—and he let the senators involved feel his wrath. Thus, Tiberius failed to manage the paradoxical situation of sole rule and Republican institutions, as he might have done had he followed Augustus's model and resorted to ambiguous communication. Instead, he acted in all sincerity, confronting the senators with contradictory demands: They were to accept him as emperor, but also act as if he did not exist, as if the Senate truly remained the real center of power, as it had been in the time of the Republic.

The difficulties that ensued as the emperor and the Roman aristocracy tried to communicate with one another in the Senate are vividly rendered in Tacitus's account of the reign of Tiberius in the *Annals*. To carry out the emperor's will without knowing what that will was required considerable skill on the part of the senators. In a telling example from the year 15, when the Senate was debating a matter of direct personal concern to him, Tiberius declared that he would vote under oath and called on the other senators to do likewise. Calpurnius Piso responded: "In what order will you register your opinion, Caesar? If first, I shall have something to follow; if last of all, I fear I may inadvertently find myself on the other side" (Tac. *Ann.* 1.74.5–6). This man known for his courage brought up the problem that usually went unmentioned, in conjunction with a clear indication of his readiness to submit to the emperor's wishes, but, as Tacitus reports, at the same time he could not avoid embarrassing Tiberius.

The situation was worsened by a change in the traditional relationships in the Roman aristocracy. These had been governed by a multi-polar system of political friendships: Friends visited one another at home for the *salutatio,* a formal morning reception, and for banquets in the evenings; they supported one another with the votes of their clients at elections or votes in the Senate; and they left each other bequests in their wills. The existence of an emperor strangely altered this situation in that there was no alternative to friendship with the emperor. All aristocrats were now the emperor's "friends" or, at the very least, no one could afford to be on bad terms with him publicly. Of course there was a distinction between those men close to the emperor, who enjoyed his particular trust, and all the rest. But the traditional forms of interaction that symbolized friendship were now extended to the entire aristocracy.

It is reported that under Augustus the entire Senate, all the members of the equestrian order, and many of the common people appeared regularly for the morning receptions at his house, turning them into a time-consuming mass event. The emperor had a decisive influence on the political offices granted to a senator, which counted as a "favor" or "kindness" (*beneficium*), an act of imperial friendship. In return the number of bequests to the emperor rose enormously, and the emperor remembered all aristocrats of highest rank in his own will. "Friendship" with the emperor thus acquired a new function, as the all-important mechanism for regulating relationships within the aristocracy. The traditional rivalries once expressed in terms of direct amity or hostility were now transformed into a competition for access to the emperor and his favor.

Here, too, Augustus had succeeded in unifying contraries by using the new hierarchical system of relationships based on the emperor's favor but behaving as if it were still the old one of close personal friendships between equals. Once again ambiguity in communication between the emperor and the aristocracy was the result. The emperor had to act as if every aristocrat were his friend, and the aristocrats pretended that they were all friends of the emperor, even though it was clear that opportunism was foremost in everyone's mind and that below the surface, feelings of genuine hostility toward the emperor existed, as became evident now and then when conspiracies were uncovered.

Tiberius is reported to have tried to withdraw as much as possible from such traditional contacts with the aristocracy and the opportunistic behavior they encouraged. Thus at his morning receptions he received the senators as a group, a step that simplified the procedure but greatly limited the possibilities for private communication with the emperor. He is also said to have systematically avoided contact with senators on other occasions, by hardly granting private interviews. Clearly he was helpless in the face of the usual flattery, which he reportedly detested.

Two central events from Tiberius's reign can be explained by his attempt to demand political decisions from the Senate that because of the altered center of power it was no longer able to make and by his withdrawal from personal communication with the aristocracy—that is, by his manner of being emperor without being willing or able to play the part required of him. These events were the treason trials and the rise of Sejanus, prefect of the Praetorian Guard.

Since under Tiberius rivalries within the aristocracy could not take the form of a competition for imperial favor that was regulated and guided from above, a new and extremely ugly form of behavior arose: intrigues and denunciation. The *lex maiestatis* had originally been applied to crimes against the "sovereignty" (*maiestas*) of the Roman polity: mutiny in the army, fomenting rebellion among the people, or gross abuse of office by magistrates. Augustus applied this law to crimes against the emperor as well, in modified form, and in the beginning Tiberius allowed such charges to be raised as a way of prosecuting the authors of vituperative attacks on him. It transpired that an aristocrat unscrupulous enough could use the charge that such a crime had been committed as a way of getting the otherwise inaccessible emperor's attention. As the aim was to appear solicitous of his safety, the more serious the alleged case, the better. At the same time the tactic provided a relatively safe way of eliminating rivals from the field. Rewards could be earned, too, since there was no public prosecutor in ancient Rome; if a defendant was found guilty, his accuser received a portion of his assets.

A typical case, reported by Tacitus, shows that allowing such charges endangered the lives of the defendants but could have a grotesque ripple effect as well. The victim in this instance was a high-ranking knight named Titius Sabinus, and his accusers were four senators of Praetorian rank. Their ambition was to become consuls, and they hoped that by pressing charges successfully against Sabinus they would win the support of his enemy Sejanus, the powerful Praetorian prefect. Lucanius Latiaris, the man on best terms with Sabinus among the four, invited him to his house and began complaining about Sejanus; he then went on to heap abuse on the emperor, and ultimately Sabinus joined in. Simultaneously the three others hid in the space between the roof and the ceiling so that they could serve as witnesses. The group then filed charges, which resulted in a death sentence and Sabinus's execution. "In Rome, the anxiety and panic, the reticence of men toward their nearest and dearest, had never been greater," Tacitus reports. "Meetings and conversations, the ears of friend and stranger were alike avoided; even things mute and inanimate—the very walls and roofs—were eyed with circumspection" (Tac. *Ann.* 4.69.3).

At the start it was often men newly raised to the rank of senator who chose this method of advancing their own careers, while their victims tended to be members of old aristocratic families whose ancestry made them potential rivals of the emperor. The crucial factor, however, was that the whole Senate heard the trials and had no choice but to condemn its own members if the emperor did not intervene. The trials thus became a process by which the aristocracy was destroying itself. Tiberius had clearly lost the ability to assess the relative importance of each case. Suetonius reports in his *Life of Tiberius* that the emperor was dominated by a dread of conspiracies—and the more trials of this nature took place, the better founded that dread seemed to be.

The increase of flattery, intrigue, denunciation, and fear among the aristocrats—to which Tiberius's own behavior unwittingly made a decisive contribution—now led the emperor to withdraw entirely from aristocratic society, and even from Rome itself. In the year 26 he moved to Campania, and the following year to the Isle of Capri. Until his death in 37 he never set foot in Rome again. It was an astonishing step: The ruler of the Roman Empire retired from Rome, the center of his realm, and from then on ran the government by correspondence. His retreat, which documented Tiberius's failure in the role of emperor, went hand in hand with the rise of Sejanus. As Praetorian prefect he was head of the emperor's bodyguard, and thus carried out an important military function. In addition, however, Sejanus possessed to a high degree the very skills so notably lacking in the emperor: He managed to his own benefit the sometimes unscrupulous opportunism that dominated aristocrats' behavior; he used the web of intrigue for his own purposes; and finally he came to monopolize the favor that Tiberius was withholding from the aristocracy.

Through clever maneuvers Sejanus had succeeded in winning Tiberius's complete trust. He achieved a position of preeminent power by the time of the emperor's withdrawal to Capri, at the very latest. He monitored the entire imperial correspondence, which was transported back and forth by the Praetorian Guard. In addition Sejanus had placed his own people in positions close to the emperor, so that he was able to oversee all access to and communication with Tiberius, and thereby controlled all avenues to gaining influence with him. As a result, the aristocrats' efforts to win the emperor's favor now became efforts to win the favor of his favorite. According to Cassius Dio's *Roman History* there was a great crush in front of Sejanus's house in Rome every morning during the *salutatio*, not only because men were afraid of being overlooked, but also because they didn't want to be seen bringing up the rear of the procession. This was true of the leaders of the Senate in particular, whose behavior was observed closely. Tacitus writes that it was possible to reach the consulship, and thereby the highest social rank, only with Sejanus's support, and the consuls themselves discussed all public and personal matters with him. At the same time, Tacitus continues, everyone who was on bad terms with Sejanus for any reason, or who stood in his way, was exposed to the gravest danger. The fate of Titius Sabinus was described above, and we will soon learn what happened to the family of Germanicus. Tiberius permitted extraordinary honors to be awarded to the commander of his bodyguard: Sejanus's birthday was celebrated publicly, and golden images of him were venerated. He reached the zenith of his power in the year 31, when he shared the consulship with the emperor, had the best prospects for marrying into the imperial family, and was promised tribunician *potestas*, which would have made him a kind of co-regent.

To trust no man but one, and trust him too much—this captures Tiberius's behavior in a nutshell. Clearly he overextended Sejanus's loyalty. Given that the question of the succession remained open, Sejanus seems to have found the temptation too great to resist: Not content with being the emperor's virtual equal, he strove to become emperor himself. The report of the conspiracy is said to have been delivered to Tiberius by a trusted slave of Antonia Minor, who as his sister-in-law had privileged access to the emperor. The old man rallied to bring off one bravura performance. He secretly appointed a new Praetorian prefect, Quintus Naevius Macro, simultaneously ordering that ships be made ready to carry him away to safety in case of emergency, to a garrison of loyal troops. Then in a dramatic denouement in the Senate, a letter was read aloud in Sejanus's presence; it began with noncommittal phrases, but finally accused him directly of plotting against the emperor. The once all-powerful favorite was executed the same day, along with his children. Their bodies were dragged through Rome for several days after that.

A new spate of trials for treason ensued, as people settled old scores and used new openings to try to make a name for themselves. In the year 33 Tiberius gave orders that everyone in prison for participating in the conspiracy was to be killed. "On the ground lay the huge hecatomb of victims: either sex, every age; the famous, the obscure," writes Tacitus, "scattered or piled in mounds. Nor was it permitted to relatives or friends to stand near, to weep over them, or even to view them too long; but a cordon of sentries, with eyes for each beholder's sorrow, escorted the rotting carcasses as they were dragged to the Tiber, there to float with the current or drift to the bank, with none to commit them to the flames or touch them. The ties of our common humanity had been dissolved by the force of terror; and before each advance of cruelty compassion receded" (Tac. *Ann.* 6.19.2–3).

At this point the relationship between the emperor and the aristocracy had reached a nadir. Both sides were extremely fearful after the events surrounding the fall of Sejanus. Those who had nothing left to lose circulated denunciations and scurrilous attacks. The emperor furnished publicity to the universal hatred that befell him, by having such tracts read aloud at their authors' indictment before the Senate. A letter Tiberius sent to the Senate, whose opening passage is cited by both Tacitus and Suetonius, vividly captures the situation near the end of his reign. It also displays the harrowing and helpless frankness so characteristic of him: "If I know what to write to you, Senators, or how to write it, or what to leave unwritten at present, may all gods and goddesses visit me with more destruction than I feel that I am daily suffering" (Tac. *Ann.* 6.6.1; Suet. *Tib.* 67.1). All communication between the emperor and the aristocracy had broken down. When the seventy-eight-year-old man, who no longer dared set foot in his home city, finally died, the Romans shouted, "Tiberius into the Tiber!" ("Tiberium in Tiberim!" Suet. *Tib.* 75.1).

A PERILOUS YOUTH

The social conditions encountered by a young man growing up in aristocratic circles in Rome during the rule of Tiberius could not have been less suited to fostering humanity. The emperor had unlimited powers and his orders had to be carried out without hesitation; at the same time he was hated and lived in constant fear of conspiracies. Many aristocrats were utterly without scruples; they would denounce each other but bow and scrape to the emperor, all the while waiting for the next opportunity to conspire against him. Murders and executions were everyday occurrences, and ultimately an ambiguity in communication with which the actual circumstances were covered over, lacking all candor and honesty, and thus further intensifying the general anxiety and uncertainty. How did Caligula fare as an adolescent in such a society?

The death of Germanicus in the year 19 rid Tiberius of a potential problem in the succession. His biological son Drusus (II) was by virtue of his age the only eligible aspirant for the throne at the time. The following years would reveal, however, that the acquisition of dynastic prestige by one branch or the other of the imperial family could always become a political problem, either because it aroused the ambitions of other family members or because third parties were able to exploit latent rivalries.

Sejanus's position as the emperor's trusted confidant made him a rival of Drusus early on. The sources report that in the year 23 he began an affair with Drusus's wife, Livilla, who was a sister of Germanicus, and persuaded her to poison her husband. Evidently the charge was clearly proved in a trial eight years later, after the Praetorian prefect's fall from favor. It is highly improbable that Sejanus had ambitions of seizing the throne himself at that time; more likely he was concerned about securing his own future if Tiberius should die. The emperor was then already over sixty, and his death would have put Sejanus in a most precarious position in the event of Drusus's succession.

After Drusus II died, the popular family of Germanicus—his widow, Agrippina, and her sons—immediately regained their central place in speculation about the succession. In a session of the Senate Tiberius particularly recommended Nero and Drusus (III), by then seventeen and sixteen years of age, to the senators, and in so doing offered official confirmation of their importance. Ten-year-old Caligula, by contrast, seemed of less interest because of both his age and his two older brothers. For a time this situation would prove a great advantage. The very next year it emerged that the senators had taken Tiberius's recommendation too literally; they heaped so many honors on Nero and Drusus that the emperor complained, perhaps because he felt a bit neglected himself. Furthermore his relationship with Agrippina was deteriorating, a development that the sources attribute mainly to intrigues set in motion by Sejanus. After the death of Drusus (II), Tiberius is said to have thought about eliminating Agrippina and her sons as well. According to Tacitus this plan failed for two reasons: The guards in the house of Germanicus's family were alert and Agrippina was too chaste for Sejanus to use his apparent charms on her. Thereupon he prevailed upon Livia and Livilla to inform Tiberius that the mother of the two possible successors was ambitious for power. Moreover Sejanus denounced her to the emperor himself, saying that Agrippina was gathering a political faction around her that threatened to divide the citizenry.

The next step—denouncing those who still dared to frequent the family's house—drew on the assistance of compliant senators. The charge was crimes against the *lex maiestatis,* as in the particularly nasty case of Titius Sabinus described above. When things went so far that even one of Agrippina's cousins was accused, Agrippina went to Tiberius to demand an explanation, and he accused her openly of a lust for power. Sejanus then made use of the atmosphere prevailing at the time, in the truest sense utterly poisoned, to mount a classic intrigue. Through intermediaries he convinced Agrippina that Tiberius was planning to poison her, and that she should avoid having anything to eat at the house of her adoptive father-in-law. When she was invited soon thereafter to a banquet at which Livia was also present, the emperor noticed that she ate nothing. (He may possibly have been informed of Agrippina's suspicions.) He praised the fruit that was just then being served, selected a piece, and handed it to her himself. This gesture only heightened her fears, so she passed the fruit to a slave in her retinue without tasting it. Tiberius is said to have turned to Livia and remarked that it would be no wonder if he were to adopt even harsher measures against Agrippina, since she thought he was trying to poison her.

If Tacitus is to be believed, Agrippina was in fact scheming to hasten her sons'—and hence her own—rise to power. If so, she would have represented a real threat to the emperor. The problem cannot be reduced to the individuals involved, however, since it was structural in nature. A very high degree of skill was required—not just of the emperor in his political role, but also of the members of his family—to master the extremely complex relationships among them, which clearly involved mistrust and intrigue. In the end it is hardly surprising that most of them would prove unequal to the task. Caligula himself represented an exception in this respect, as time would show.

The next victim was his eldest brother, Nero, who had become the leading candidate for the throne after the death of Drusus (II). A marriage had been arranged for Nero with his cousin Julia, who was Drusus's daughter and thus a granddaughter of Tiberius. The household he thus acquired seems to have been instrumental in his downfall. "In spite of the modesty of his youth"—thus Tacitus characterizes the syndrome of inadequacy described above—Nero "too often forgot what the times demanded" (Tac. *Ann.* 4.59.3). Tacitus reports further that Nero's freedmen and clients were hoping to gain influence themselves if he became emperor, so they urged him to show vigor and confidence. The people and the army were behind him, they said, and Sejanus, who was now exploiting the trust of the aging emperor, would not dare to make a move against him. The Praetorian prefect had covert informants placed in Nero's house, however, and they carried any incautious remark elicited from Nero straight to Sejanus and the emperor. Nero was not even safe at night, for whether he was awake, or slept, or sighed, his wife, Julia, supposedly told her mother, Livilla, about it, and she passed the information on to her lover Sejanus. For his part Sejanus now fed the feelings of rivalry and envy in Nero's brother Drusus (III), whom he won over and encouraged in his hopes for the throne. The time was ripe in the year 27, when Nero was twenty-one and Tiberius already settled on Capri: Agrippina and her eldest son were placed under arrest. Soldiers were assigned to guard them; to watch over all their activities and contacts, including the letters and visitors they received; and to report everything they said.

These events, to which the fourteen-year-old Caligula was an immediate witness, meant that a new home had to be found for him and his two young sisters, Drusilla and Livilla. (Their sister Agrippina married shortly thereafter.) The three children moved into the house of their great-grandmother, Livia, the widow of Augustus who as grande dame kept up associations with many aristocrats and had a corresponding degree of influence.

She is supposed to have intervened to prevent Agrippina and Nero from being placed on trial and condemned. She died two years later, at the age of eighty-six, and Caligula appeared in public on that occasion and delivered her funeral oration. Once again it was necessary for Germanicus's children to seek a new home. In the year 29 Caligula and his sisters moved to the house of their grandmother Antonia Minor, the other grande dame in Rome during that era. Antonia was well connected not only in Rome, but also in the East. Through her father, Marcus Antonius, and his relationship with Cleopatra, she had ties to several rulers there, who functioned as "client kings" of Rome, and their families. Several princes were also living in Antonia's house at the time and got to know Caligula; later on the relationship would stand them in good stead.

Caligula's stay in Antonia's house was destined to last only two years. During this period—as Sejanus's power was approaching its peak—the final downfall of his mother and eldest brother occurred. The emperor himself had written a letter accusing them of various crimes. Because of a gap in Tacitus's *Annals* and the abbreviated accounts of Suetonius and Cassius Dio, their trial before the Senate cannot be reconstructed in detail. But if we do not know which senators aided Sejanus in instigating it, we do know its outcome: Nero was declared *hostis,* an enemy of the Roman polity, and banished to the island of Pontia; Agrippina was exiled to the island of Pandateria. The circumstances of Nero's death on Pontia—probably in the year 30—remain unclear; he may have been starved to death or have killed himself, possibly driven to suicide because he believed he was about to be executed: Suetonius reports that an executioner was sent to Nero to show him the noose and hooks.

In that same year Caligula's brother Drusus (III), who stood next in succession to the throne, came under attack from Sejanus and his minions. Like Nero he was accused of conspiring against the emperor. For years agents had shadowed and eavesdropped on him as well, activities in which his wife, Aemilia Lepida, is said to have played an important role. Caligula, at that time seventeen or eighteen years old, witnessed how Drusus was thrown into a dungeon on the Palatine Hill, from which he would never emerge. Not much later he too was declared a *hostis;* in his trial the senator Lucius Cassius Longinus served as prosecutor, a role that earned him Sejanus's goodwill.

There is little reason to doubt what the sources say about how the members of Germanicus's family were eliminated. In part the authors based their accounts on sessions of the Senate, for which minutes were available to them. The violent deaths of Caligula's mother and brothers are thus firmly established. It is unclear, however, what was going through Tiberius's mind in those years. Suetonius asserts in hindsight that Tiberius had planned to kill the members of Germanicus's family from the start and simply used Sejanus to carry out his will. This claim attempts to explain the brutality of their deaths, but it is not very plausible. According to Cassius Dio, people had concluded Tiberius was mad, because he ultimately brought up the details of their deaths before the Senate, giving himself away completely. It must be assumed that the emperor had lost a sense of reality as he suffered constant fear for his own safety; the fear was actually heightened by his withdrawal from Rome and the influence, on Capri, exerted by his immediate environment, which Sejanus was controlling. In Rome fear must have been the dominant emotion in the Senate as well, for otherwise it is impossible to explain the senators' reaction to the detailed reports about how Agrippina, Nero, and Drusus were spied upon: Although in fact they were appalled at the emperor's behavior, as Tacitus reports, they pretended that what horrified them was the supposed enmity within the imperial family.

It took no great skill for Romans to figure out who was next in line, and accounts exist of several attempts to eliminate Caligula, too. Later, after the fall of Sejanus, several senators were prosecuted for attempting crimes of this kind. Sextius Paconianus was alleged to have helped the Praetorian prefect to organize an intrigue against Caligula. Cotta Messalinus and a close confidant of Tiberius named Sextus Vistilius were accused of having spread rumors about his dissolute morals. (Allegations of sexual misconduct had also played a role in the case against Nero.) Everything suggested then that Caligula would soon be placed on trial as well, but things took an unexpected turn.

CAPRI AND THE PATH TO THE THRONE

Toward the end of the year 30, that is to say before the dramatic downfall of Sejanus the following October, described above, Tiberius summoned the eighteen-year-old Caligula to Capri. Only now was he granted the *toga virilis,* the formal sign identifying him as an adult. The man's toga suggested that the emperor was considering him as a possible successor. But what were the aging emperor's real intentions for him? Evidence suggests that at first Caligula had a different role to play. The purpose of the young man's presence on Capri was to make the emperor safer: In effect his status closely resembled that of a hostage.

Several events at this time indicate that in dynastic terms the prestige of Germanicus's sons remained high or had even risen because people felt pity for them. When the Senate took action against Agrippina and Nero, a rebellious crowd had surrounded the Curia, where the senators were in session, carrying pictures of both and demanding that they be spared. And during the planning for the overthrow of Sejanus, Macro had instructions that if the action failed, he was to fetch Drusus from his dungeon and present him to the people. The idea was that if the need arose they might be able to exploit Drusus's popularity in order to shift power back to their side. Finally, it is also reported that the mood in Rome turned against Sejanus and the prefect gave up his plans for a coup the moment that Caligula was summoned to Capri and appeared to be gaining in favor with the emperor. Taking into his household the remaining son of Germanicus, on whom no suspicion had as yet been cast, was a clever tactical move on Tiberius's part—or on the part of his new strongman, Macro. Caligula's popularity could help to stabilize the emperor's own position, and bringing him to Capri would deprive others of the opportunity to make him their instrument.

A new phase of life began for Caligula, but one that was no less dangerous than before. From now on he had to live close to Tiberius, the man responsible for sending his mother into exile, imprisoning his brother Nero, and killing Drusus. The emperor's attitude toward Caligula must have been ambivalent at best. Without doubt the people closest to the emperor were hostile toward Caligula, and most of them had played more or less leading roles in the proceedings against the other members of his family. For them the prospect of Caligula's accession to the throne must have looked ominous. One man in this circle, Aulus Avillius Flaccus by name, is described as enjoying the confidence of both the emperor and Macro; beginning in the year 32 he would become governor of Egypt, one of the highest positions available to a knight. He and several other men envisioned an alternative solution to the succession: Tiberius had a biological grandson, Tiberius Gemellus, from the marriage of his son Drusus (II). The boy, also on Capri at the time, was only twelve years old in the year 31, but because the emperor was showing no signs of infirmity, Gemellus presented a realistic and considerably better option for the future to Flaccus and his associates. Under such circumstances Caligula's own fate must have looked uncertain, and it is reasonable to assume that his actions were dominated by one motive—to survive. His position would remain precarious for six more years, until his actual elevation to the throne in the year 37 put a temporary halt to the threats.

At first the situation on Capri must have been overshadowed by events in Rome, where as a result of Sejanus's downfall the trials and executions for treason were reaching a peak among the aristocracy. The death of Sejanus had no positive effects at all on Caligula's family, however. His brother Drusus (III) starved to death in his prison on the Palatine in the year 33, reportedly after trying to eat the hay used as stuffing in his mattress. The circumstances of his death became known because Tiberius wanted to justify his treatment of Drusus to the Senate and therefore ordered the reports of the spies in Drusus's household and of his prison guards to be read aloud. It emerged from the accounts that Augustus's great-grandson had been beaten by slaves after begging for food and attempting to leave his cell, and that at the end, although weakened to the point of apathy, he had uttered dreadful curses against Tiberius. Agrippina died that same year, a suicide according to the official version, although people suspected that she too had been starved. How did Caligula react to the deaths of his mother and second brother and Tiberius's responsibility for them?

Tacitus reports: Caligula's "monstrous character was masked by a hypocritical modesty: Not a word escaped him at the sentencing of his mother or the destruction of his brothers; whatever the mood assumed for the day by Tiberius, the attitude of his grandson was the same, and his words not greatly different" (*Ann.* 6.20.1). Suetonius's account is similar: "Although at Capri every kind of wile was resorted to by those who tried to lure him or force him to utter complaints, he never gave them any satisfaction, ignoring the ruin of his kindred as if nothing at all had happened, passing over his own ill treatment with an incredible pretense of indifference, and so obsequious toward his grandfather and his household that it was well said of him that no one had ever been a better slave or a worse master" (Suet. *Cal.* 10.2).

Here it is necessary to distinguish between factual information and moral value judgments in the accounts written after Caligula's death. Above all it is essential to be clear about the character of these judgments. Tacitus, in no uncertain terms, condemned the fearful hypocrisy and submissiveness displayed toward the emperor by even the highest-ranking and most powerful members of the aristocracy. And we know that Caligula's mother and brothers had been brought down by their own incautious comments about Tiberius, passed on by spies placed in their households. Yet despite this state of affairs Tacitus demands from the nineteen-year-old Caligula a forthrightness and sincerity that would have been extremely foolish and would certainly have cost him his life.

If we leave aside the double moral standard, what remains is this: In contrast to his mother, his brothers, and other members of the imperial family in the preceding years, and in spite of the emperor's unpredictability and the open hostility of people around him, Caligula managed to maintain his position. The price he paid for this was to control his own feelings and to play a part in front of Tiberius. He possessed an advantage, however. Philo of Alexandria, who, as the leader of a Jewish delegation, met Caligula twice, described it. Although Philo mostly heaped abuse on

Caligula in hate-filled tirades, in this passage, inconsistently with his usual antipathy, he reports that Caligula "was skilled in discerning a man's secret wishes and feelings from his open countenance" (Phil. *Leg.* 263).

The degree of danger posed by the situation on Capri is demonstrated vividly by two episodes. One involves Julius Agrippa, a grandson of Herod the Great who had grown up in the house of Antonia Minor in Rome. In the year 36 he received permission to visit Tiberius. He was asked to accompany Gemellus, the emperor's grandson, on his excursions, but instead began spending time with Caligula, whose favor he hoped to win. When they had become better acquainted and were out for a drive one day, Agrippa expressed the wish that Tiberius would make way for Caligula on the throne as soon as possible, since the young man was so much worthier of it. The driver of the carriage, a freedman of Agrippa's, overheard the remark, and when he was accused of stealing some clothing a little later, he reported it to the emperor, citing Agrippa's exact words: "I hope that the day will at length arrive when this old man will leave the scene and appoint you ruler of the world. For his grandson Tiberius would by no means stand in our way, since you would put him to death. The world would then know bliss, and I above all" (Jos. *Ant.* 18.187). Tiberius believed the man, and the prince, despite his purple robes, was arrested on the spot and led away in chains. For Caligula, who had not allowed himself to be drawn out even in a very private setting, the episode had no repercussions.

Another instance of the dangers of Capri involved Tiberius's favorite companions, for, according to reports, he most enjoyed the society of Greek philosophers, grammarians, poets, and astrologers. At meals he would carry on learned conversations with them, raising questions that had occurred to him in his daily reading. As could be expected, given that he was not simply another scholar but the emperor of Rome, there was naturally great competition for his favor. Gaining it could mean fame and riches, but the pursuit was also dangerous, as the companions vying for it used every means at their disposal. Suetonius writes that the grammarian Seleucus inquired of the emperor's servants what their master was reading, so that with advance preparation he could dazzle Tiberius with his knowledge. Unfortunately, he seems to have overdone it. The emperor, already weary of the opportunistic behavior of aristocrats in Rome, detested it even more in his inner circle on Capri, so when his suspicions were aroused he looked into the matter. Seleucus was banned from his daily company and later forced to commit suicide.

Caligula apparently had more success when he took part in the learned discussions on Capri. We are told that he had a profound knowledge of the works with which educated men of the day were expected to be familiar. Josephus writes that "he was, moreover, a first-rate orator, deeply versed in the Greek and Latin languages. He knew how to reply impromptu to speeches that others had composed after long preparation, and to show himself instantly more persuasive than anyone else, even where the greatest matters were debated. All this resulted from a natural aptitude for such things and from his adding to that aptitude the practice of taking elaborate pains to strengthen it." There is no question that he had enjoyed a good education from his earliest years. As was customary in aristocratic families, Caligula probably received instruction from tutors, who were usually Greek slaves or freedmen. He may have been influenced by the reported interest of his father, Germanicus, in scholarship and literature, or perhaps his interest was spurred by his journeys as a child to the centers of ancient learning in Greece and Egypt. It appears that he also made use of his time on Capri to further his studies. According to Josephus again: "Being the grandson of the brother of Tiberius... he was under a great compulsion to apply himself to education, because Tiberius himself also had conspicuously succeeded in attaining the highest place in it. Gaius followed him in his attachment to such noble pursuits, yielding to the injunctions of a man who was both his kinsman and his commander-in-chief" (Jos. *Ant.* 19.208–9).

No accounts of the later period of Caligula's rule mention a particular interest in learning. It is thus probably no mistake to assume that in this respect, too, he skillfully adapted his behavior on Capri to the prevailing circumstances and showed an interest in the subjects Tiberius preferred, especially since he was clearly endowed with the requisite intellectual gifts. And he did improve his relationship with the emperor, which was no doubt quite strained to begin with because of the general political atmosphere and the particular family constellation. At least their relationship appears to have grown better during Caligula's first two years on Capri. Although Tiberius did not display any particular friendship to his great-nephew and potential successor, neither was he openly hostile.

In the year 33, that is, in the same period when his mother and remaining brother met their deaths, Caligula was appointed quaestor, the lowest honorary political office, which carried with it automatic membership in the Senate. He was only twenty, under the usual minimum age for the quaestorship. At the same time he was given permission to be a candidate for other offices, five years before reaching the required age. This was a privilege traditionally granted to princes of the imperial family and could thus be interpreted as a positive signal for his position. And finally Tiberius had arranged for Caligula to marry Junia Claudilla (or Claudia) during a visit to Antium. She was the daughter of Marcus Junius Silanus, a former consul who had gained attention by introducing servile and flattering resolutions in the Senate. He was considered one of Tiberius's closest associates and received the right to cast his vote first. This was an extraordinary honor that gave him the highest standing in the Roman aristocracy. In political terms such an honor was not without its dangers, as shown by the emperor's behavior in the Senate described above. Nevertheless Silanus was clearly able to use his standing skillfully.

Caligula's marriage would last only a short time, and it is impossible to determine how much it meant to him. Nor can anything positive be deduced from it about Tiberius's plans for the succession. Each of Caligula's brothers had been married to a cousin (Nero to Julia, a granddaughter of Tiberius, and Drusus to Aemilia Lepida, a great-granddaughter of Augustus) and thereby gained the prestige conferred by an additional connection with the ruling family. No further young ladies of appropriate background were available, but the idea that one of these might take Caligula as a second husband seems not to have been considered. Julia was perhaps excluded because her testimony had contributed to Nero's downfall. Aemilia Lepida might have been a candidate, for her participation in the fall of Drusus (III) was not discussed until years later, but both women remarried aristocrats unconnected to the imperial family. Caligula's wife, Junia Claudilla, could boast of no comparable ancestry. Nor did the marriages of his sisters, which were certainly based on the emperor's plans, reveal any particular favor. Only Agrippina the Younger married Gnaeus Domitius Ahenobarbus, a grandson of Marcus Antonius and Octavia, Augustus's sister. The later emperor Nero was the offspring of this marriage. Drusilla was married to Lucius Cassius Longinus, descended from an old aristocratic family, while Livilla's husband, Marcus Vincius, came from a less illustrious background. Tiberius's marriage policy with regard to the children of Germanicus and Agrippina can thus be summed up as follows: None of the marriages he arranged had the slightest effect on the possibility that his own grandson, Tiberius Gemellus, might become emperor.

Caligula's future remained uncertain, since no doubt he stood in the way of Tiberius's biological grandson, because of both his own descent and his popularity in Rome. During his stay on Capri he was further awarded two religious offices that were a customary part of a Roman senator's career, but they also permit no conclusions about the emperor's plans for him. Finally, in the year 35, Tiberius drew up a will, whose contents can be described as most definitely leaving both options open. Caligula and Gemellus received equal shares of his inheritance, in a decision that was no decision at all. Even at that point, however, the conclusion that emerged two years later upon Tiberius's death must have been evident. The imperial office was not divisible, yet according to the will the vast imperial assets would have had to be divided, even though by this time they constituted a central part of the emperor's authority and had taken on a character that in the modern sense of the word was public and no longer private. If it is not to be read as documentary evidence that Tiberius was incapable of making up his mind—in which case the emperor could have dispensed with it entirely— then the message it conveyed was clear: The question of the succession was to remain open.

In addition to Caligula's indifference to the fate of his family and his successful opportunism in dealings with the emperor and his circle, Suetonius reports that during his time on Capri the later emperor was already unable to conceal his brutal and depraved character. Caligula "was a most eager witness of the tortures and executions of those who suffered punishment, reveling at night in gluttony and adultery, disguised in a wig and a long robe, passionately devoted besides to the theatrical arts of dancing and singing, in which Tiberius very willingly indulged him, in the hope that through these his savage nature might be softened. This last was so clearly evident to the shrewd old man that he used to say now and then that to allow Gaius to live would prove the ruin of himself and of all men" (Suet. *Cal.* 11).

It is easy enough to assess this account if one takes into consideration the general situation as it is reported in other, unjaundiced passages that do not touch on Caligula. From Tacitus's account, cited above, we know that after the death of Sejanus the demeanor of those present was carefully observed when guilty sentences were announced or executions were carried out, in an attempt to discern any indication of hostility toward the emperor. Any such sign perceived in a person's reaction was reported. Thus if Caligula was present at executions on Capri—an occurrence reported nowhere else—he was probably under close observation also. Not too much significance for interpreting his character should be attached to his failure to display much emotion. Furthermore, no evidence survives, written or archeological, to suggest the existence of taverns, brothels, or theaters on the island at that time. Or to put it more precisely: The milieu on Capri was not that of a large city like Rome, where it was easy to move about incognito. Furthermore, there are no indications that on occasional visits to the mainland Caligula would have been able—or would have wanted—to absent himself from the emperor's entourage. Suetonius has thus ascribed to him attributes reported from the youth of a later emperor in Rome who was similarly hated, namely Nero. Finally, the suggestion that the old emperor saw through Caligula's deception explicitly contradicts reports by Suetonius himself and others of Caligula's ability to dissimulate, which he had perfected and which probably saved his life on Capri. It also contradicts everything that can be inferred about Tiberius's own personality from accounts of his behavior over many years. Tiberius's most notable trait was placing too much trust in one person (Sejanus) and responding with exaggerated distrust to everyone else; if he had one failing, it was precisely the lack of what is claimed for him in this passage: a sound knowledge of human nature. Suetonius's account is thus utterly false. He has projected alleged qualities of the later "evil" emperor Caligula back into the time of his residence on Capri.

For Caligula's ultimately successful path to the imperial throne, the support of Macro, prefect of the Praetorian Guard, was decisive. All the sources are unanimous on that point. They also agree that intrigue was involved, as was only to be expected in view of the emperor's failure to settle on a successor. Exactly how this intrigue played out cannot be determined, but that very fact suggests its secrecy was well planned—whether by Caligula himself, by Macro, or by Ennia, the prefect's wife.

After Junia Claudilla died in childbirth, Caligula and Ennia are supposed to have begun an affair. Philo reports the "widespread view" that because she had a sexual relationship with Caligula she was able to persuade her husband to defend her lover when others denounced him to Tiberius, and also to support Caligula as an aspirant to the throne. If this version is correct, then the intrigue probably originated in Ennia's ambition to become empress. According to Suetonius, however, Caligula seduced

Ennia and promised to marry her, so that she would intervene with Macro and gain his backing. Tacitus, and similarly Cassius Dio, reports a third version, that it was Macro who attempted to win Caligula's favor by inducing Ennia to have an affair with him, hoping that a bond with the wife would also extend to the husband. This last version is certainly the most implausible. It presumes that Caligula's succession was a foregone conclusion, regardless of whether Macro supported him or not, so that Caligula would have had no reason to seek Macro's favor. Macro, however, is generally depicted as the most powerful man of that day after the emperor.

It is difficult to assess the situation because we do not know how often Macro visited Capri, where Ennia must have spent considerable time. Her relationship with the future emperor probably was not sexual at all, and the married couple was simply paving the way for Caligula's succession through a division of labor—with Macro machinating in Rome and Ennia on Capri in the role of Caligula's confidante. Such an interpretation would fit well with the harmonious relationship among the three in the first few months after Caligula's accession to the throne. Yet whatever the details of the intrigue were, it involved bypassing the emperor and his grandson to contrive the succession. It was an extremely risky enterprise, but again Caligula prevailed.

He seems to have remained in danger until the very end, however. Several sources report that Tiberius was concerned for the safety of his grandson, then seventeen years old, if Caligula should become emperor. Philo writes that Macro saved Caligula's life several times on Capri; he also mentions reports that Caligula would have been eliminated if Tiberius had lived only a little while longer, for very serious allegations had been raised against him. These charges may refer to the intrigue concerning the succession. According to Philo, toward the end of his life Tiberius was planning to name his biological grandson as his successor. Dio tells a different story: Tiberius considered Gemellus illegitimate, the child of Livilla's liaison with Sejanus, and therefore he preferred Caligula. Josephus provides yet another version, that Tiberius decided to regard a chance occurrence as an omen and indicator of God's will. The conflicting accounts suggest that the succession was an open question until the last moment. Tacitus probably came closest to the truth when he concluded that Tiberius could not summon the strength to make a decision.

Tiberius died on 16 March in the year 37. In the preceding weeks the old man had approached the city of his birth for the last time, but he died at Misenum, the base of the Roman fleet. Various rumors about his death found their way into circulation. According to one, after death seemed to have occurred and preparations were already under way to proclaim Caligula emperor, Tiberius is supposed to have regained consciousness suddenly and asked for food. While everyone else present stood rooted to the spot in terror, Macro ran into the bed chamber, threw covers over the emperor, and smothered him. Another version declared that Caligula had hastened his adoptive grandfather's demise, first with poison and then by strangling him with his own hands. According to a third account, Caligula had first starved the emperor and then suffocated him with Macro's help. Regardless of how the emperor actually died, even in their diversity the reports of the death of the emperor—who over the years had become ever more odious—confirm the contemporaries' image of the center of power, where Caligula had lived for six years: All who took part were in mortal peril.

The same day, members of the Praetorian Guard in Misenum proclaimed Caligula *imperator*. Following arrangements with the consuls and leading senators, the Roman Senate accepted the new disposition of power. On 18 March Tiberius's last will and testament was set aside on the grounds that he had been of unsound mind when he made it. The Senate—an ancient and honorable institution that in the preceding two decades had both lost a large number of members to violence and suffered a decline in morale—recognized the son of Germanicus as emperor in absentia. After his arrival in Rome on 28 March, "the right and the power to decide on all affairs" was conferred on him (Suet. *Cal.* 14.1). With this step Caligula, at the age of twenty-four, became Gaius Caesar Augustus Germanicus and ruler of the Roman Empire.

TWO

Two Years as *Princeps*

A YOUNG AUGUSTUS

The journey from Misenum to Rome took ten days. As the young emperor, dressed in mourning, accompanied the body of Tiberius, he received striking demonstrations of sympathy from the population. "His progress was marked by altars, victims, and blazing torches, and he was met by a dense and joyful throng, who called him, besides other propitious names, their 'star,' their 'chick,' their 'babe,' and their 'nursling'" (Suet. *Cal.* 13). Germanicus's prestige and popularity had survived the reign of Tiberius and were now transferred to his remaining son—in more intense form because the other family members had met such tragic fates. Suetonius reports that Caligula was "the emperor most earnestly desired" (*exoptatissimus princeps*) by the inhabitants of the provinces and by the soldiers who had known him as a child, just as he was also by the whole population of the city of Rome (Suet. *Cal.* 13). When he entered the capital, the center of the ancient world in which he had not set foot for the past six years, the celebrations

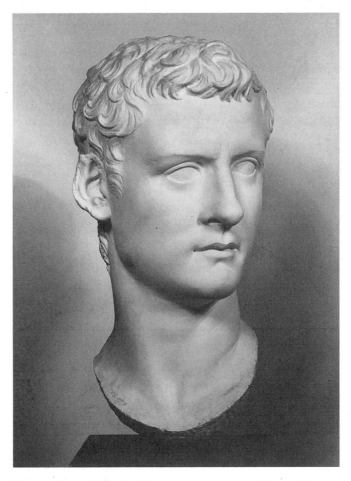

Figure 3. Bust of Caligula. Worcester, Massachussets, Museum of Art, Acc. 1914.23.

are said to have gone on for almost three months, and more than 160,000 animals were sacrificed—and eaten.

But how did the aristocracy react to the twenty-four-year-old new ruler? Would the flattery, denunciations, and intrigue continue as they had under Tiberius? And how would the young Augustus behave toward the senators? It was from their circle, after all, that the criminal charges against his mother and brothers had originated, and the Senate as a whole had pronounced the verdicts against them. After nearly seventy years of sole rule under Augustus and Tiberius, it had become evident that an emperor's success or failure rested above all on the delicate business of communicating with his fellow aristocrats.

Caligula's first step was to deliver a speech at a session of the Senate to which representatives of the equestrian order and the people had been invited. According to Cassius Dio's account, he flattered the senators, promising to share his power with them and to do all he could to please them. He even referred to himself as their son and ward. Specifically, he announced that he was putting an end to trials for *maiestas,* which had had such dreadful effects on the aristocracy and its relationship with the emperor. All those who had been exiled or imprisoned under Tiberius would regain their freedom, Caligula declared. He ordered all the documents connected with those trials, which his predecessor had preserved and which also concerned the charges against his mother and his brothers, to be publicly burned in the Forum (not without securing copies of them first, as it would later transpire). This was an effort to assuage the fears of senators and knights who had played a prominent role in the trials, and to close this terrible chapter of the past. Caligula emphasized his intention truly to begin anew by his reaction to the first denunciation for conspiracy he received: He ignored it, and declared that he could have done nothing to arouse anyone's hatred. He would pay no heed to informers.

How to commemorate the deceased emperor was another question. As Tiberius's adopted grandson and successor Caligula had to preserve the proper degree of respect for his memory, but the dominant attitude in the Senate was still detestation. In his first written communication to the Senate Caligula had requested that Tiberius be granted the same honors that Augustus had received after death, elevation to the status of a god and inclusion in the Roman pantheon. The senators had not overcome their reluctance to comply with this request before the new emperor's arrival, but neither had they taken the opposite step (which would no doubt have reflected their feelings more accurately) of officially condemning his memory (*damnatio memoriae*) and thereby expunging him from the public records. Caligula let the matter rest, in an undecided state that certainly matched the personality of the deceased; the body lay in state and was then buried in Augustus's mausoleum in an elaborate public ceremony. Delivering the funeral oration, the new emperor mainly recalled Augustus and Germanicus and placed himself in their tradition.

Caligula then proceeded to honor Tiberius's bequests—even though his will had been declared invalid. The members of the Praetorian Guard received 1,000 sesterces each, roughly the annual pay of an ordinary soldier. Forty-five million sesterces were paid out to the people of Rome; the urban cohorts, a kind of police force, and the firemen, who also exercised paramilitary functions, each received 500; and every citizen soldier in the Empire was given 300 sesterces. In addition the new emperor ordered distribution of the bequests in Livia's will, which Tiberius had ignored after her death eight years earlier. Finally Caligula added his own contribution: He doubled the amount for the

Praetorian Guard, and granted 300 sesterces to the head of every family in Rome. The money that rained down on the citizens of Rome at Caligula's accession left a lasting impression of his generosity, a virtue loved above all by soldiers and the urban plebs, and one that made emperors popular.

The payments to the Praetorian Guard allowed Caligula to provide a striking reminder of his own power. Before the assembled Senate, he inspected his bodyguards, who had sworn an oath of loyalty to him. It was not lost on the spectators at the drill that the officers and men under Macro's command were largely the same men who had not so long ago, on the orders of the previous emperor or Sejanus, arrested, tortured, or beheaded no small number of their Senate colleagues.

A further symbolic act honored the members of Caligula's immediate family who had predeceased him. Despite stormy seas Caligula sailed at once to the islands where his mother and brother had died, exhumed their remains himself, and brought them back to Ostia, Rome's port. From there he had them transported up the Tiber to the city by ship. At midday, when the streets were most crowded, prominent knights carried the two urns through Rome on litters normally used for transporting statues of gods. The procession ended at the Mausoleum of Augustus, where the remains were interred. The whole ceremony was arranged to resemble a delayed triumph for the family of Germanicus: A field marshal's standard flew from the stern of the ship, and Caligula wore a purple-bordered toga and was accompanied by lictors, as if he himself were a victorious commander. It was decreed that an image of his mother, Agrippina, mounted on a carriage, would henceforth accompany all festival processions. The month of September was renamed after Germanicus, who joined Julius Caesar and Augustus as the only men so honored.

These extraordinary honors for the dead were complemented by others for the living members of Caligula's family. The Senate granted to his grandmother Antonia Minor the title Augusta and all the further marks of distinction once given to Livia. The emperor chose his uncle Claudius, who until then had received no attention at all, to serve with him as co-consul during his first term in that office. And on behalf of his sisters Drusilla, Agrippina, and Livilla he decreed that the following sentence be included in all public oaths: "I will not hold myself and my children dearer than I do Gaius and his sisters" (Suet. *Cal.* 15.3). The sisters were further awarded the privilege of sitting with him in the emperor's box when they attended games at the Circus. Lastly, Caligula adopted Tiberius Gemellus, only some seven years younger than himself, and granted him the *toga virilis* along with the title "Prince of the Youth," which Augustus had given to the grandsons whom he intended to make his heirs. Thus Caligula's co-heir and rival for the throne, who had been passed over when Tiberius's will was set aside, became his son—and the favored candidate to succeed the brand-new emperor.

Next Caligula renounced honors for himself or any acknowledgment in public of his unique status. He forbade statues of himself to be erected within the city of Rome, and abandoned Tiberius's custom of sending letters to the Senate and people; such letters had long before acquired the force of official directives, so that to continue them would have belied Caligula's stated intention to share power. Finally he let three months pass before assuming the consulship on 1 July 37. Despite depleted political significance, the consulship remained the highest regular office in Rome, and had been held several times by Augustus and Tiberius during their rule, for the distinction it conferred. By postponing his entry upon the consulship Caligula prevented the two men in office from having to resign. His stint in office, which lasted only about two months, enabled the two senators who had been next in line for the honorific positions to fill them for the remainder of the year.

When he did take up the office of consul, Caligula used the occasion to deliver a policy speech in the Senate, for the first time explicitly distancing himself from Tiberius. He criticized all the actions that had earned his predecessor the enmity of the aristocracy, and announced a number of provisions for his own rule, including concessions. These corresponded so closely to the senators' own wishes that, as Cassius Dio reports, "the Senate, fearing that he might change his mind, issued a decree that this speech should be read every year" (Dio 59.6.7). Otherwise Caligula's brief first consulate consisted largely of magnificent festivities, which reached a climax with the formal dedication of the temple the new emperor had completed for his great-grandfather, the deified Augustus. All the senators and their wives along with the people of Rome were invited to a banquet in the city, and games were held on an unparalleled scale. Four hundred bears and the same number of beasts of prey from Libya were killed in combat in the arena, and chariot races allowed young aristocrats to display their most dashing form. Caligula himself appeared driving a triumphal chariot drawn by six horses, "something that had never been done before" (Dio 59.7.4). The emperor also took advantage of his first consulate to simplify the rules of protocol. He abolished a ritual that had upheld the ruler's unique status, the customary greeting to an emperor in the city, and from then on appeared in the role of a simple citizen—at least as far as ceremonial greetings were concerned.

The first few months of Caligula's reign can be clearly seen as an attempt to copy the Augustan Principate—a development that his contemporaries in the aristocracy no doubt registered with satisfaction. On the level of official politics his sole rule was not in evidence; rather he insisted that power was shared between the *princeps* and the Senate. He paid strict attention to the proper forms of communication between the emperor and the aristocrats in the Senate, which had traditionally symbolized their equality. He avoided any display of honor due to his position of political power in everyday social encounters. Within the city Caligula insisted upon forms of address befitting an ordinary (aristocratic) citizen; the Romans praised this as an example of *civilitas,* civic and unassuming behavior. On the other hand Caligula was unmistakably the sole ruler. He alone commanded the armed forces, a fact that every senator could observe when the Praetorian Guard went through its drills. He used his financial means, far superior to everyone else's, to make gifts of money and hold games, fostering a sense of obligation among soldiers and the common people in general. He found clever ways to augment the family prestige accruing to him through his descent, which helped to solidify his position as emperor.

All this meant was that Caligula resumed the ambiguous form of communication that had been established under Augustus (and later collapsed under Tiberius) to disguise the simultaneous existence of an aristocratic republic and autarchy. The Senate resolution requiring that Caligula's speech as consul be recorded and read aloud annually reveals tellingly how aware the senators were of the situation and how complex all communication became as a result. It shows that they knew power was shared at the emperor's pleasure and the arrangement could be rescinded at any time—in other words, that power was not really shared at all. Yet they could neither directly express their distrust of the emperor's declaration that he would share power, nor openly try to force him to keep his word, since either action would imply that his promise was empty. They had to take the indirect form of awarding him an honor. On its manifest level the Senate resolution said: The emperor has given such a momentous and important speech that it deserves to be read aloud every year. At the same time, however, the honor latently revealed that emperor had not truly shared power, for otherwise it would not have been necessary to remind him of his obligation in this way.

That the senators were adept at this form of communication is not surprising. But where did Caligula learn it? How could some- one without the least experience in institutional Roman politics have possessed such a perfect command of it from the start? How had his ability to present himself as an Augustan *princeps* developed? Clearly the role had been well thought out, and Cal- igula played it well. Who advised him on the matter?

Philo identifies Macro and Marcus Junius Silanus as the men behind the young emperor. As Praetorian prefect Macro held the highest office possible for a knight, and Silanus, Caligula's former father-in-law, had the highest standing in the aristocracy because of his seniority among the senators. Both men had advanced to their positions under Tiberius; they belonged to the inner circle of power, and their management had smoothed Cal- igula's elevation to the throne. Dio reports that Macro arranged the Senate's approval in advance with the two consuls and "others"; Silanus's status must have ensured that he was included. We may safely assume that the configuration of Caligula's rule had been discussed in this circle and concessions made to any men or groups who were reluctant.

Macro and Silanus are also supposed to have guided the young emperor after his elevation. Of the former Philo writes:

"Knowing... that he had saved Gaius over and over again when within an ace of destruction [i.e., on Capri], he gave his admonitions frankly and without disguise, for like a good builder he wished his handiwork to remain proof against destruction or dissolution either by himself or by another" (Phil. *Leg.* 41). Macro advised Caligula how an emperor should behave at aristocratic banquets or at theatrical performances for the common people, and also gave him lectures on the art of governing: "The fittest contribution for a ruler is to put forth good proposals for the benefit of his subjects, to execute these proposals in the best way possible, and to bring forth good gifts with a bountiful hand and will" (Phil. *Leg.* 51). Silanus played a similar role: "In all his discourse, he talked as a guardian, concealing nothing that might tend to improve and benefit Gaius's character, conduct, and government. He had, indeed, strong inducements to speak freely in his preeminently noble lineage and his close connection by marriage. For his daughter had died only a short time before; the rights of her kinsfolk had grown faint... but some last remnants of their vitality still existed" (Phil. *Leg.* 63).

As for Caligula's share in his Augustan Principate, all that can be said is that he played the role to perfection. Though indubitably better than before his elevation to the throne, his situation continued to be anything but simple. The two manipulators who had made him emperor had cemented their own positions of power at the same time and were hardly about to give them up voluntarily. Furthermore by adopting Gemellus he had created an abiding rival for the throne. Thus the two powerful men behind the throne always had an option open; there was an alternative to Caligula.

ILLNESS AND CONSOLIDATION

As in other pre-modern monarchies, the advent of a new ruler in ancient Rome frequently bred conflict at the center of power— structural conflict, intensified through generational differences. Would the trusted entourage of the old emperor adjust to the new one? They owed their rise and influence to the old ruler and had not been chosen by the new one; their position was indepen- dent of his favor, at least in the beginning. Typically a new ruler gathered his own close confidants around him; these began as rivals of the inner circle from the old regime and then pushed them aside. The rearrangement could be an adaptation, or it could be a great upheaval.

Caligula's closest confidants were his sisters—who shared with him not only ties of blood but also the experience of great danger under Tiberius; the husband of one of them also belonged to the inner circle. Caligula felt extraordinary affection for Drusilla especially. Tiberius had arranged her marriage to Lucius Cassius Longinus, but they were now divorced; her second hus- band, Marcus Aemilius Lepidus, belonged to the same generation as the siblings. Lepidus came from a high-ranking family with its own ties to the imperial house, and he was Caligula's closest con- fidant among the aristocracy. What kind of relationship would develop between this circle on the one hand and Macro and Sila- nus on the other?

A resolution developed more quickly than might have been expected. In the eighth month of his reign, at the end of October 37, Caligula fell gravely ill. No information has survived about what the disease was. The population of Rome was alarmed and grieved. Large crowds are said to have demonstrated their concern for the young emperor by surrounding the Palatine Hill every night, waiting for news. What would happen if he died? Who would succeed him?

All the known events of the next few weeks allow the following conclusion to be drawn: Macro and Silanus, the two leading men, seized the initiative. In case Caligula should die, they conferred with a number of people and prepared the way for Tiberius Gemellus, the only possible successor in the existing dynastic constellation. This was the only rational strategy, the only one that fit the circumstances, although they obviously set about implementing it a little too soon. Any other choice would have encouraged the ambitions of aristocratic pretenders to the throne and risked an outbreak of violent conflict. A crisis had developed sooner than anyone could have anticipated. Caligula's adoption of Gemellus had been strategic, but laden with possible future difficulties. It would constitute a problem if he were to have a biological son or wish to name someone else as heir. In the meantime, however, there was no alternative to Gemellus, and this meant that if Caligula died, his sisters and Aemilius Lepidus would lose their unique position and the power attached to it; conceivably even their personal safety might be threatened.

In this situation Caligula first seized the initiative as emperor. From his sickbed he named his favorite sister, Drusilla, to inherit the imperial "property and the throne" (*bonorum atque imperii;* Suet. *Cal.* 24.1), in effect making Lepidus his successor. As soon as he regained his health, he laid a plan that was brutal but under the circumstances only logical: to eliminate Tiberius Gemellus, who as long as he lived would remain a magnet for conspirators hostile to the emperor and ambitious to place their own man on the throne. Gemellus was accused of plotting against Caligula, of having counted on his death and attempted to profit from it. A centurion and a military tribune were dispatched and forced him to commit suicide. Philo vividly describes the tragic scene: Since Gemellus had no experience of warfare and had never witnessed a suicide, he had to be instructed in the technique, "and having received this first and last lesson he was forced to become his own murderer" (Phil. *Leg.* 31).

The loss of an established candidate for the succession weakened Macro and Silanus. Not long afterward, probably at the start of the year 38, it was the turn of Macro and his wife, Ennia, to fall from power. To replace a Praetorian prefect was an enterprise fraught with danger, but nevertheless it was achieved smoothly in two steps. First the emperor appointed Macro prefect of Egypt, the second-highest office in the Empire for a knight, and replaced him not with one man but with *two*. Caligula was following Augustus's model: Since the man in charge of the emperor's bodyguard always represented a potential threat, Augustus had named two to the position at a time, ensuring that they would be rivals for power and keep an eye on one another. Caligula seems to have chosen the appointees wisely. They were men plucked from obscurity (only one, Marcus Arrecinus Clemens, is known by name) and owed a particularly great debt to the emperor as a result.

Before Macro could embark for Egypt, he and many other people were charged with crimes and then either executed or forced to commit suicide. In Philo's words, Caligula began to "fabricate charges against him, which though false were plausible and readily believed"; on one count Macro had supposedly claimed that Caligula was a creature of his making and that the emperor owed the throne to him (Phil. *Leg.* 57–58). Some were found guilty on the basis of witnesses' testimony and the evidence from earlier trials, supposedly destroyed, that they had participated in attacks on Caligula's mother, his brothers, and their supporters. Others were accused of behaving inappropriately during the emperor's illness. The charges suggest that the main targets were old enemies of Germanicus's family who had hoped for Gemellus's accession and presumably acted accordingly. One such man was Avillius Flaccus, who lost his office as prefect of Egypt in the autumn of 38.

Then it was Silanus's turn. It sufficed for the emperor to indicate his displeasure with him in the Senate. Caligula altered the procedure so that the former consuls would vote in order of seniority, thus terminating Silanus's privilege as highest-ranking senator. Everyone who had lived through the reign of Tiberius realized that it was only a matter of time until some unscrupulous senators would bring charges against the man whom Caligula had publicly demoted. Silanus saw the handwriting on the wall and committed suicide, enabling his family to retain his fortune, since if he had been tried and found guilty it would have been confiscated.

Judged by the standards of a modern society in which political disagreements and power struggles are conducted without violence, Caligula's elimination of the people who had helped him secure the throne, and particularly his treatment of young Gemellus, were reprehensible. Given his experience of life near the throne, however, he may well have felt he had a stark alternative: Either them or me and my family. From the perspective of today this assessment can hardly be termed incorrect, and contemporaries concurred with it. Philo, whose aim is otherwise to stress Caligula's immorality, cites at length opinions that ran counter to his own appraisal:

"Of his own cousin and fellow heir they would talk thus: 'Sovereignty cannot be shared; that is an immutable law of nature. He being the stronger promptly did to the weaker what the weaker would have done to him. This is defense, not murder. Perhaps, too, it was providential and for the benefit of all mankind that the lad was put out of the way, since some would have been partisans of him and others of Gaius, and it is such things that create disturbances and wars both civil and foreign.'... Of Macro they said, 'His pride extended beyond reasonable limits... What reason had he for reversing his part and transferring the subject to the rank of ruler, and Gaius, the emperor, to the place of a subject? To command, which is what he did, befits best the sovereign, and to obey, which is what he deemed Gaius should submit to, befits the subject'... In the case of Silanus, the argument ran, 'he was under a ridiculous delusion in thinking that a father-in-law had the same influence over a son-in-law as a real father has over his son... But this silly man, even though he had ceased to be a father-in-law, extended his activities beyond his sphere and did not understand that the death of his daughter carried with it the death of the matrimonial affinity'" (Phil. *Leg.* 67–71).

Together with the elimination of the emperor's last rival for power, the two most powerful men in his circle, and old family enemies, other measures shed light on the difficulties and dangers of the transitional period. Shortly after recovering his health Caligula married for a second time, indicating that he intended to father an heir and provide for a dynastic succession. His chosen bride was Livia Orestilla, whom he is said to have obtained by high-handedly abducting her during her wedding to another man, Gaius Calpurnius Piso. Supposedly Caligula justified his behavior by the examples of Romulus and Augustus, each of whom chose to wed a woman who was already married. Augustus had even married Livia while she was pregnant. Livia Orestilla behaved quite differently from her predecessor of the same name. This aristocratic young woman appears to have had no interest in being empress—a status for which others would have been prepared to suffer a good deal more than abduction. She remained loyal to the husband she had chosen herself, and had unauthorized contact with him, thereby effectively disqualifying herself for the task intended for her of giving birth to legitimate imperial offspring. A short time afterwards, the marriage ended in divorce, and Orestilla was banished from Rome, although the surviving accounts provide contradictory details. Calpurnius Piso's admission to the distinguished priestly college of the Arval Brethren in May 38 suggests that Caligula's choice of bride was accomplished less sensationally, or at least that it occurred with the consent of her former bridegroom and thus conformed to Roman custom.

Some of Caligula's other measures, political in the narrower sense, were more successful. At the New Year oaths were usually sworn to uphold the decrees of previous emperors; in the year 38 Tiberius was excluded, in a nod to the Senate, which had desired to expunge his memory. In addition Caligula rescinded Tiberius's ban on the historical writings of Titus Labienus, Cremutius Cordus and Cassius Severus, announcing that he attached great importance to full historical records for later generations. He also reintroduced the custom of publishing and presenting to the Senate the *rationes imperii,* the accounts of the officials responsible for administering military and financial matters in the Empire. Because the relationship between the emperor's own assets and the public treasury was a complex one, it is unclear exactly which outlays were included, but in any case the measure corresponded well to his announced intention of sharing rule with the Senate. Further innovations were aimed at the judicial system. Caligula limited the legal cases that could be appealed to him as emperor, a move to enhance the importance of work done by judges of senatorial rank. He created a fifth *decuria* or panel of judges to expedite hearing cases. And finally the emperor carried out a long overdue reform of the equestrian order, expelling unworthy members and admitting new ones, with special attention to high-ranking and wealthy officials of cities around the Empire. To many of them he granted the privilege of wearing senatorial rather than equestrian insignia of rank, even though they were not members of the Senate.

For all of Italy Caligula waived the general sales tax, which had probably been earlier reduced to one half of one percent. This measure benefited the lower classes above all. A return to the old procedure for electing magistrates was aimed at the people of Rome. Under Tiberius these elections had been removed from the popular assemblies and given to the Senate. The change had made it easier for the emperor to exert control, had relieved senators of ruinous campaign expenses, mostly from sponsoring games. Cassius Dio makes it clear that the aristocracy responded to the revival of popular elections with skepticism. The emperor's goal may have been to restore the advantages the common people enjoyed when candidates had to try to win their favor. The measure had no noticeable effect in the political sphere, however, since there was rarely more than one candidate for any given office. The voters paid so little attention to the reinstated electoral process that Caligula was forced to abolish it later. Presumably the renewal of permission to found *collegia* was also granted as a boon to the plebs. These were corporations and social clubs, and sometimes economic ventures as well, most of whose members came from the lower classes; they had been banned during the late Republic for political reasons. Caligula held lavish gladiatorial games whose cost in both blood and money was extravagant. And finally he had the floor removed from the *Saepta*—originally a gathering place for elections—and flooded it, so that naval battles could be presented there. It was later replaced by a wooden amphitheater.

Most of the political measures introduced early in the year 38, around the time that Macro and Silanus fell from power, were enthusiastically received. The Senate responded by voting special honors to the emperor. Every year on a particular date, for example, a golden bust of Caligula was to be carried to the Capitol, with the entire Senate marching in the procession and boys and girls from the leading senatorial families singing songs in praise of the emperor's virtues. The first day of Caligula's reign was designated *Parilia* like 21 April, the date of Rome's founding, implying that he had founded the city anew.

Caligula's policies were undoubtedly aimed at reconciling the various politically relevant populations to his rule. A clear difference emerges, however, from earlier actions at the time of Macro and Silanus, which still bore the stamp of the Augustan Principate. Caligula accommodated the Senate—which continued to look to the ideal of the "free" Republic, now long gone—by making the finances of the Empire public and by changing the appellate procedure for legal cases, but he also took the Republican ideal seriously in instances where it jarred with the senators' interests. Historians could circulate their works uncensored in keeping with the notion of Republican freedom, but there were disadvantages. As Tacitus showed in his account of Tiberius's reign in the *Annals,* a frank account of past events documented not only the emperor's despotism but also the unscrupulous opportunism of some senators and the submissiveness of the Senate as a whole—discreditable behavior which the Senate would have preferred forgotten. Reintroduction of popular elections for magistrates was similarly two-edged. Elections were a fundamental element of the Republican political order, but they had been contrary to the interests of the senatorial aristocracy for some time. Now that the Empire was administered by the emperor, senators had lost their former opportunities for enriching themselves as administrators in the provinces. Because many senators could thus no longer run exorbitant election campaigns, they had come to terms with holding elections in the Senate, though it was tantamount to appointment of magistrates by the emperor. Caligula's renewal of old traditions outdid the Senate in its conservatism and simultaneously forestalled its objections; the senators could not criticize without exposing the selectivity in their glorification of the past, so that they were forced to remain silent.

In his ingenious positioning vis-à-vis the Senate, Caligula at the same time made good use of his support among the plebs, who profited more than the aristocracy from his political and economic changes. The emperor was not afraid to give the lower classes greater scope for political action through popular elections and *collegia*. He elevated upper-class inhabitants of the provinces to the equestrian order and smoothed their path to the Senate by awarding them the symbols of senatorial rank in advance. All this was definitely in the emperor's own interest as well. As already apparent under Augustus, "new men" who were indebted to the emperor for their advancement to the Senate tended to be considerably more compliant than members of the old aristocratic families (at least in the first generation). The changes were presented, however, as a return to the good old ways, an aim that no senator could publicly oppose.

The political measures accompanying the removal of Gemellus, his supporters, and the two leading figures from the reign of

Tiberius were thus clever and astute. They furthered the interests of the senatorial aristocracy, the equestrian order, the upper class in the provinces, and the plebeians in Rome itself, while also strengthening the emperor's hand. It is probably a credit to them that no threat to Caligula's position emerged in the period immediately following.

How much was Caligula himself responsible for these successful efforts to consolidate power and how much should be ascribed to his advisers? It is difficult to know. A number of people besides Lepidus, Drusilla, Agrippina, and Livilla probably influenced him, and the two new Praetorian prefects and other senior officers of the imperial guard undoubtedly played an important role. Individuals like King Julius Agrippa, who is supposed to have been on friendly terms with the emperor, and perhaps a few senators presumably turned their proximity to him to account. Finally, probably already active behind the scenes was a group whose significance would not become evident until later—the freedmen who acted as secretaries and administrators in the imperial household. Such men were employed in all large aristocratic households, and because of their dependent status and specific skills they often possessed important specialized knowledge that their noble masters were unwilling or unable to acquire themselves.

A hint of Caligula's own personal stamp on the measures described above is provided by a strange episode immediately after his illness. A Roman citizen named Afranius Potitus had sworn a vow to offer his own life if the emperor recovered, while a knight named Atanius Secundus had vowed that he would fight as a gladiator. After regaining his health Caligula insisted that both men fulfill their promises, to keep them from perjuring themselves. Instead of receiving the rewards they had hoped to obtain by their exaggerated devotion, both met their deaths. Caligula's reaction is telling. It has affinities with his measures in 38 and typifies behavior to emerge in crasser form more and more frequently as time passed. Caligula began, like Augustus, by enjoying flattery, but this changed after the first few months of his reign. He did not respond like Tiberius, however, seeking to avoid flatterers by withdrawing from the public sphere entirely. Instead, Caligula framed a new response to the ambiguous communication that had become normal in dealing with the emperor. The two men's vows were ambiguous in that the explicit wish—for the emperor's recovery—did not match the unstated wish—to be rewarded for their flattery. Caligula showed that he would abjure this form of communication, by taking it at face value. One could say that he simply outed them. He attributed to their utterances a sincerity that they could not deny without admitting that the emperor's health had not been foremost in their minds—and the consequences of such an admission were foreseeable.

In Caligula's dealings with the Senate after the fall of Macro and Silanus too, he took the declared ideals—derived from the old Republic—at face value and implemented them. This contravened the real interests of men who had professed the ideals, but they could not complain without losing face. The principle behind the emperor's actions was cynical, but not without wit of a kind. At this point it took fairly harmless form, apart from the fate of Afranius and Atanius. Later, however, the principle would operate in much more unpleasant forms.

HOLDING POWER

Never before had Rome been ruled by a young man. For centuries a handful of experienced older men, the *principes* of the

Roman aristocracy, had been the leaders and made the decisions. The first two sole rulers, Julius Caesar and Augustus, had won their positions by victories in protracted civil wars and were middle-aged when they began to govern. Tiberius had been a successful general in the provinces for many years before he became emperor at the age of fifty-four. Now the question was: How would a young man measure up? Caligula came from a prestigious family, certainly, and had survived the webs of intrigue spun around the old emperor, but he had no experience at all in politics. How would the aristocracy, led as always by old men of great experience, deal with a young man on the throne?

A provisional answer has already been given. At first Caligula played the part of an Augustan *princeps,* but then went on to secure his power by eliminating his rivals. He took specific measures to stabilize his position as ruler with different segments of the population, without making too many concessions to the aristocracy. The nobles seemed to find this acceptable. The situation remained fluid, however, because of an aspect of politics omitted in our discussion thus far: Politics in ancient Rome was not limited to specifically political institutions like the Senate, the magistracy and—for a time under Caligula—the popular assemblies. In fact the household, which the Romans called "private" and which they contrasted with the *res publica,* was itself a scene of politics. In Rome the private sphere was in a certain sense also public, and the political sphere operated to a large extent through personal relationships.

During the Republic the houses of the Roman aristocracy had developed into informal centers of communication, where political action took preliminary shape before being introduced in official bodies. Reciprocal visits at morning receptions and evening banquets both constituted and manifested the personal relationships, linking those who appeared at these events as friends or clients. Patronage structured the relationships. Participants helped each other in the law courts, in money matters, and in elections and political disputes. They left each other legacies. There were clear rules for the support friends and clients owed one another, rules that made the participants' behavior predictable and reliable. The size of an aristocrat's household, along with the number and rank of the friends and clients who met there, affected his chances for exercising real power in the institutional sphere, in politics in the narrower sense. The material luxury in such households was politically relevant, too. Carved marble ornamentation, costly paintings and furniture, gold and silver tableware, the lavishness of the food and entertainment offered at banquets—all these attested to the owner's wealth and potential value as a patron, his social status, and the political influence he possessed or felt entitled to claim. Aristocrats took precise note of the size and opulence of each other's houses and tried not to fall behind in the competition.

Just like sessions of the Senate, gatherings at aristocrats' homes were regulated by ceremonial customs illustrating the political and social rank of the participants. In the case of the morning *salutatio,* visitors' status and their relationship to the host were reflected in the rooms they were permitted to enter and the order in which he greeted them. Banquets were typically attended by nine people ranged around a table on three banqueting couches with different levels of prestige. The importance of these ceremonial customs, which may seem alien from the perspective of today's largely egalitarian society, is shown in the conflicts that arose when they were not observed.

But how should an emperor organize his household? Who should be received at home, in what luxury and according to which ceremonial rules? How should the emperor shape his "personal" relationships with aristocrats? As noted above, Augustus and Tiberius had set virtually no precedents. Their desire to keep the emperor's actual status as far in the background as possible had led to preservation of the old customs to a large extent, even though they were becoming increasingly impracticable. The emperor's house was small, the furnishings modest, and the crush at the *salutatio* great, since on certain occasions the entire aristocracy appeared. Because banquets remained limited to the usual size, Augustus was obliged to give them "constantly," often arriving late and leaving early due to other demands on his time. During the last years of Tiberius's rule when he was living in seclusion on Capri, no imperial "household" had existed in Rome any more at all. So how was the new young emperor to run his house? Should he keep it as it was, below the standards of size and sumptuousness long since adopted by the rest of the aristocracy? Should he regularly admit all senators and the most prominent knights to morning receptions? Should he surround himself with venerable old men at evening banquets and make sure that their respective ranks were reflected at the table?

Tiberius had left more than two billion sesterces at his death. He thus offers a prime demonstration that frugality by itself could not make a Roman emperor popular. It is reported that Caligula went through this sum and more in either one year (Suetonius) or two (Cassius Dio). Most was undoubtedly spent on the immense gifts he made to soldiers and the people of Rome at the start of his rule, but a considerable portion seems to have flowed into running his household as well. His household expenditure reached a level far exceeding the aristocrats'. He began extensive construction on the Palatine Hill, enlarging the complex of freestanding houses belonging to the emperor in the direction of the Forum, so that most of the hill—the most prestigious residential area in Rome—was now reserved exclusively for his use.

Caligula built extensively outside Rome as well, on a much grander scale than his fellow aristocrats. Villas and palaces in rural settings raised previous efforts to incorporate nature and dominate the landscape to a new level. Caligula tried to realize plans that others considered impossible: "He built moles out into the deep and stormy sea, tunneled rocks of hardest flint, built up plains to the height of mountains, and razed mountains to the level of the plain, all with incredible dispatch" (Suet. *Cal.* 37.3). For sea journeys he had galleys built "with ten banks of oars, with sterns set with gems, particolored sails, huge, spacious baths, colonnades, and banquet halls, and even a great variety of vines and fruit trees; that on board them he might recline at table from an early hour and coast along the shores of Campania amid songs and choruses" (Suet. *Cal.* 37.2).

It is striking that on the subject of the morning *salutatio* at Caligula's house, only a single account exists—although it reveals that the ceremony took place regularly. Philo notes that King Julius Agrippa came "to pay his wonted respects" during his visit to Rome and that others were present (Phil. *Leg.* 261). The odd dearth of information can probably be attributed to later efforts by senators in particular, who had been obliged to be "friends" of the emperor, to obliterate their contacts with him from the record as far as they could; the aristocratic sources reveal traces of such alteration in other contexts as well. Thus it is not certain whether Caligula performed the expected ceremonial rituals during the first two years of his reign or not. He clearly did not behave in the expected manner at banquets, which were extremely lavish yet at the same time informal.

Early on Macro is supposed to have cautioned the young *princeps* not to show too much enjoyment in the music and dance offered as dinner entertainment, and certainly not to participate; he should not snigger like a boy at coarse jokes or fall asleep during the banqueting, as none of this befitted the emperor's dignity. Later Caligula ignored the usual protocol for seating guests: His sisters lay on the couches to his right, the places normally given to a wife and children, while his wife was permitted to lie to his left in the place of honor. When his uncle Claudius arrived late he could obtain a place only with effort and after several attempts.

Besides criticizing violations of traditional etiquette at the emperor's banquets, the sources also find fault with the people he invited. Caligula enjoyed the company of the Greens faction of chariot racers at the Circus Maximus, for example, visiting their building as a guest himself and inviting the well-known charioteer Eutychus to a banquet, at which he gave the racer a gift of two million sesterces. Nonetheless senators continued to covet an invitation to dine with the emperor as a particular honor. Reports mention the presence at banquets of the sitting consuls, of aristocratic ladies with their husbands, and of Vespasian, the later emperor, who was Caligula's guest during his praetorship and even showed his gratitude with a flattering speech in the Senate.

While the ceremonial rituals for guests of high rank were flouted, the aristocrats invited to imperial banquets were witnesses to enormous outlays of money. Foods were served covered with gold leaf; entirely new dishes might be created for the occasion, and Caligula himself is said to have drunk vinegar in which valuable pearls had been dissolved. All of this is condemned in ancient sources (and often in modern accounts as well) as more or less pointless luxury and waste. Display of this kind had a definite function, though, in the context of aristocratic competition for status and thus also a latent political dimension. As mentioned earlier, members of the senatorial and equestrian orders engaged in competition over the luxury of their houses and the number and status of people who frequented them. This competition seems even to have increased with the establishment of imperial rule and the aristocracy's loss of real power—that is to say, it became compensatory. Tacitus reports that in the period from the start of Augustus's sole rule to the death of Nero huge sums were squandered on luxury: "The more handsome the fortune, the palace, the establishment of a man, the more imposing his reputation and his clientèle" (Tac. *Ann.* 3.55.1–2).

The sources often recount aristocratic extravagance. Caligula's later wife Lollia Paulina, for instance, is reported to have appeared on a not particularly festive occasion wearing jewelry worth forty million sesterces (forty times the minimum wealth qualification for senatorial rank). She did not even owe these fabulous jewels to her status as empress but had inherited them from her father. The pearls dissolved in vinegar had a special story behind them: Cleopatra was said to have made a wager with her lover Marcus Antonius that she could spend ten million sesterces on a single meal, and won the bet by drinking pearls in vinegar. The luxury and extravagance in Caligula's household signified his unattainable, quasi-royal superiority in the only area where aristocrats could still vie with the emperor. In fact, Tacitus reports in the passage just cited that families belonging to the old Republican high nobility, the so-called *nobilitas,* wealthy and famous in years past, had ruined themselves with their pursuit of conspicuous luxury.

Caligula flouted many expectations of how a Roman aristocrat ought to conduct himself in public. His decision to dispense with elaborate ceremonial greetings was welcomed, certainly, and made it easier and simpler to encounter him in the streets and squares of the city. Yet he behaved more informally than suited the tastes of the upper classes. Macro's admonitions to the young emperor about not showing too much enthusiasm at Circus games or theatrical performances were in vain. Caligula became an active supporter of one of the four factions at the Circus Maximus. His passion for chariot races was such that he built his own stadium, called the *Gaianum,* in the gardens on the Vatican Hill, where he could drive chariots himself. Aulus Vitellius, son of a man of consular rank, who would later become Roman emperor himself for a few months, shared the same passion, acquiring the special favor of Caligula and also, if Suetonius is to be believed, a limp as the result of an accident. Caligula's enthusiasm for gladiatorial combat, both between men and against animals, went so far that he trained and fought with gladiators, and is even supposed to have used real weapons. The emperor also had a great love for the theater. He surrounded himself with stars of the stage, including the actor Apelles, who became part of his retinue for a while, and the famed mime Mnester, with whom he spent so much time that it was later claimed the two had a homosexual relationship.

In his passion for chariot races, gladiatorial games, and theatrical performances Caligula shared the interests of contemporary young aristocrats. Since Augustus, the youth of the noblest families in Rome had sometimes participated in chariot races, athletic competitions, and combat with wild animals at the Circus, together with gladiators from the equestrian order. The sons of senators who took part in a gladiatorial game put on by Caligula must have had some training in this kind of combat. Games in Rome were by no means just entertainment; they had a political dimension. It was significant *that* the emperor presented games, and also *how* he did so. The city's arenas were the most important spaces for direct communication between the emperor and the urban plebs. Approval or criticism was communicated to the emperor during games through cheers or booing. Quite frequently chanting choruses of sports fans pressed demands that direct confrontation made it hard for the emperor to reject. Attending the contests, he showed solidarity with the people and allowed them to observe him at close quarters. When Augustus attended games at the Circus "he gave his entire attention to the performance, either to avoid the censure to which he realized that his [adoptive] father Caesar had been generally exposed because he spent his time in reading or answering letters and petitions; or from his interest and pleasure in the spectacle, which he never denied but often frankly confessed" (Suet. *Aug.* 45.1).

Throngs of young Romans were devotees of Circus games and the theater, and the people liked it when the emperor attended. Caligula, however, seems to have offended notions about proper public behavior for an emperor. He took sides himself for or against certain actors, and grew angry if the audience didn't join in or applauded performances of which he did not approve. He was "so carried away by his interest in singing and dancing that even at the public performances he could not refrain from singing with the tragic actor as he delivered his lines, or from openly imitating his gestures by way of praise or correction" (Suet. *Cal.* 54.1). From the perspective of the aristocracy his conduct meant that the young man who had become their ruler behaved "like one of the crowd" (Dio 59.5.4).

Caligula's organization of his household and his behavior in public were thus inconsistent with the role he played in institutional politics. While the latter showed moderation and skill and was generally praised, in the former he presumed upon his special status to the full. His displays of extravagance relegated the opulence of aristocratic houses to second class, and his unconventional manners at home flouted aristocrats' preference that distinctions of rank be respected. His enthusiasm for the Circus and personal ties to actors and charioteers further violated aristocratic proprieties. At home he exalted himself above his fellow aristocrats, whereas in public he fell short of the dignity befitting an aristocrat, let alone an emperor. Various reasons can be suggested for this conduct: The years on Capri had removed him from senatorial society and provided too little aristocratic socialization, while the years of oppression and danger led him to savor his imperial possibilities, which must have seemed virtually unlimited. Last but not least, the role his predecessors had bequeathed to him was only imprecisely defined. The question now was, how would the Roman aristocracy react to Caligula's behavior in the long term? There had never been a young, extravagant emperor with a passion for the arena in Rome before.

THE DEATH OF DRUSILLA

On 10 June 38 Drusilla died unexpectedly—the sister who had always been Caligula's favorite and whom he had named as sole heir. He found her loss so extraordinarily painful that he could not bring himself to attend the elaborate public funeral with which she was honored. Seneca wrote critically that just as he was unable to show joy or pleasure in a manner suitable for an emperor, he was unable to mourn appropriately. Caligula shunned human company in Rome and withdrew to his country estate in the Alban Hills, where he tried to distract himself with dice and board games. Then he traveled aimlessly around the region, letting his beard and hair grow in grief.

Caligula granted Drusilla unusual posthumous honors. On top of all the honors Livia had received after her death, the Senate passed a measure deifying Drusilla, an honor previously granted only to Julius Caesar and Augustus. A gold portrait of her was placed in the Curia, and in the Temple of Venus on the Forum a statue of her was erected the same size as the statue to the goddess herself. Drusilla was also to receive her own temple, for which a new college of priests would be established. When women took an oath, they were to use her name, as the emperor did from then on, swearing by the divine Drusilla. Great games would be held on her birthday. In the cities of the Empire she was to be venerated as Panthea, the "All-Goddess," and we know from inscriptions in the Greek part of the Empire in the East that these instructions were carried out. In Rome, the regulations on mourning were enforced with extreme rigor. Visits to the thermal baths and banquets were prohibited. One man who sold water to mix with wine is supposed to have been executed for the crime of *maiestas*. The senator Livius Geminus declared under oath that he had witnessed how Drusilla rose to heaven and conversed with the gods, vowing that he wished to be struck dead along with his children if he were lying. In contrast to similar attempts when Caligula was ill, the flattery succeeded and the senator was rewarded with a million sesterces.

Seneca writes that people were uncertain whether the emperor would prefer for them to mourn his sister or to worship her, and he describes Caligula's actions as immoderate in the extreme.

Modern authors have also declared his behavior strange, and even speculated that he may have suffered a nervous breakdown. Without any doubt he was very deeply affected. The claim that his grief was excessive may be unwarrantable, however, since the deification of a male ruler had precedents and Drusilla was Caligula's designated successor. Her deification was the first time a woman from the imperial family was added to the Roman pantheon, but not the last. The same distinction was granted to Livia under Claudius and to Poppaea Sabina during the reign of Nero.

The unusual honors bestowed on Drusilla after her death were also intended to augment the prestige of the dynasty, and Caligula's behavior immediately afterwards was entirely rational. The question of the succession was once again completely open, a situation that could lead to dangerous instability if the emperor should fall ill, as the previous year had shown. A few months after the death of his sister Caligula therefore married again. His choice fell on Lollia Paulina, a woman famous for her beauty and, as noted above, her great wealth. She was already married to Publius Memmius Regulus, a man of consular rank who at that time was governor of Moesia, Macedonia, and Achaea. According to Suetonius, Regulus is supposed to have suggested the marriage to Caligula himself and agreed to the divorce, yet even this should not be regarded as abnormal. Marriage within the aristocracy was a tactic in families' political planning, rarely correlated with personal attraction or love. For sex a Roman senator had ample choice of extramarital partners among both freedwomen and slaves. The connection to the emperor Regulus would gain from Lollia Paulina's marriage was undoubtedly worth more to him than remaining married to his wife. He was present in Rome himself for the wedding and retained his provincial office into the reign of Claudius.

This marriage did not last long either, however. Caligula ended it, presumably in the summer of the following year. Cassius Dio writes that "allegedly" the wife was infertile, but the real reason was that Caligula was tired of her. Tacitus's reports on the year 48 show that the reason given out was in fact true: When the emperor Claudius wanted to remarry, the very same Lollia Paulina was recommended to him with the endorsement that because she had borne no children she would create no complications for the imperial family. The high-born lady still possessed all the qualities of an empress ten years later and was actually infertile. Caligula's separation from her was thus by no means the result of mere whim. But the marriage did have an unintended but probably inevitable secondary consequence: Aemilius Lepidus, who had spent almost a year with the prospect of possibly succeeding to the throne, now knew that Drusilla's death and Caligula's remarriage had put an end to this chance once and for all. Events a year later, however, would show that he had not resigned himself to the fact.

THE EMPIRE

The Roman Empire, conquered during the centuries of the Republic, formed the basis of the Roman emperors' power. Their untold wealth flowed from taxes collected in the provinces, and their political power was supported by the military forces stationed there (along with the elite troops and the paramilitary groups who kept order in Rome). At the same time, however, the resources of the Empire constituted a potential danger for the emperor. High-ranking members of the senatorial order governed nearly all the various provinces. These men were responsible for law and order in their regions and carried out administrative and jurisdictional tasks. They were in charge of the legions stationed there, whose commanding officers were Roman senators as well. A long tradition decreed that only members of the senatorial order, men of high social standing and political experience, could be considered for leadership positions in the Empire. The emperor, whose rule always drew latent rivalry from his fellow aristocrats, thus had to depend on precisely those fellow aristocrats to administer his rule. The military forces in the Empire, the base of his dominant position since the civil wars of the late Republic, could be used to threaten his grip on power in a crisis. In addition to choosing the "right" men for crucial posts, meaning primarily ones who were not of too noble birth, there were two main strategies an emperor could use to preempt crises and, in a countermove, use the Empire to stabilize his own position: He could strengthen his personal relationship with soldiers, and he could heighten his activities as a patron toward the populations of the provinces—meaning above all toward the municipal aristocracies of the Empire. Both strategies required him to spend money, but ideally they also demanded his presence in person.

The last time an emperor had traveled to one of the provinces lay almost half a century in the past, when Augustus had visited Gaul. Tiberius had not left Italy once during his entire reign. Caligula, who had already greatly favored the upper classes in the provinces when he expanded the equestrian order, spent a lot of time abroad, particularly in view of the brevity of his rule. A few weeks after Drusilla's death, in about the middle of the year 38, he departed on a journey to Sicily. He began construction on a large port terminal with granaries near the city of Rhegium, so that ships arriving from Egypt could unload their cargoes of grain there. Presumably this helped to supply southern Italy, and in Josephus's view it represents the most useful act of Caligula's reign. On his visit to the city of Syracuse, the emperor sponsored games, presumably in honor of Drusilla, and had repairs made to its dilapidated walls and temples.

Seneca, Suetonius, and Cassius Dio do not mention the harbor construction at all, and note the journey to Sicily only in passing. For the city of Syracuse, however, the event was probably the most significant in its recent history. As we know from other instances, an emperor's visit was an occasion for great festivities with elaborate greeting ceremonies and many honors conferred on the ruler by city leaders and the entire population. By sponsoring games and construction projects and making extensive gifts in return, the emperor raised his profile as a benefactor, a role to which the Syracusans would refer on later occasions. It appears that other Sicilian towns also received the honor of a visit. Caligula is reported to have left Messina ahead of schedule because Mount Etna was threatening to erupt.

On his return he began by concentrating on further benefits for Rome. In October he joined his Praetorian guards in putting out a fire; the emperor's personal participation attracted general attention. In the year 38 he also began construction of two new aqueducts, the Aqua Claudia and the Anio Novus, to bring water to Rome from Tibur (modern Tivoli). Both ambitious projects were completed by his successor, Claudius.

Finally, preparations must have begun in this year for a large-scale campaign in Germania. In 39, legions and supplementary troops were assembled from all over the Empire; extensive recruiting efforts took place everywhere, and huge amounts of food and other supplies were stockpiled. Between 200,000 and 250,000 soldiers are said to have been involved. These preparations may also have included plans to build the new town in the Alps mentioned by Suetonius. The campaign was a response to incursions into Gaul by Germanic tribes from east of the Rhine; the decisive impulse, however, was probably the young emperor's wish to recommence the conquest of Germania his father had pursued and win military glory for himself. Success in war remained the most important source of prestige in Roman society; it could both increase the emperor's support among soldiers and widen the gap in status between him and the aristocracy. Through his wars in Spain between 27 and 24 B.C. Augustus had demonstrated that campaigns could enable an emperor to sidestep conflicts at home and benefit from a victory abroad to solidify his position in Rome. The emperors appreciated the significance of military fame for enhancing their position. In imperial Rome, celebration of a triumph, a distinction traditionally granted to victorious generals in the field, became reserved with few exceptions exclusively for the ruler, who officially exercised supreme command. Thus the preparations for war indicate that Caligula was making a concerted attempt to use the resources of the Empire to consolidate his own position.

The plans for the campaign in Germania were drawn up in conjunction with other measures in the Greek and eastern parts of the Empire. There was a string of Roman-dominated client kingdoms extending from the Bosporus through Thrace and Syria to Palestine, some of which Tiberius had brought under Roman administration as a result of domestic political upheavals and the spread of Parthian influence. In the year 37 Caligula had already placed two kings on the throne, Julius Agrippa in Judaea and Antiochus IV Epiphanes in Commagene, and had supplied both with substantial gifts of funds. Both of them had spent part of their youth in Rome and continued to reside there after their coronations. Agrippa, who had been in close contact with Caligula since his time on Capri at the latest (but possibly as early as his stay in the house of Antonia), was even granted the insignia of Praetorian rank by the Senate after Caligula became emperor.

At the end of the year 38 Caligula granted further territories in Asia Minor and the Near East. Three sons of Cotys, the king of Thrace—Rhoemetalces, Polemon II, and Cotys, who as great-grandsons of Marcus Antonius and Cleopatra had family ties to the emperor—were granted kingdoms, as were Sohaemus, the scion of an indigenous princely family, and Mithridates, a great-grandson of the famous Mithridates VI. Taken together their kingdoms stretched from the region of the Black Sea to Lesser Armenia. Caligula had these grants confirmed by the Senate, and formally installed the kings himself in solemn ceremonies on the Rostra in the Forum. It is possible that Caligula envisioned these new client kingdoms as part of more extensive plans for the eastern regions of the Empire. Thus it is reported that he intended to rebuild the palace of Polycrates on Samos and also to dig a canal through the Isthmus of Corinth. Both projects would have aligned him vividly with the traditions of Hellenistic kings, and also with the great dictator Julius Caesar, who had made the most recent attempt to create a canal there (following the Corinthian tyrant Periander and King Demetrius Poliorcetes of Macedonia). More will be said below about Caligula's plans for a journey to Alexandria and the East, which took on more definite shape two years later and owed much to the example of his father, Germanicus.

What sort of picture would the Roman senatorial aristocracy have had of Caligula, then twenty-six years old, toward the end of the year 38? How did all his varied activities fit together? Within a short time he had acted directly and without scruple to rid himself of both rivals for the throne and of Tiberius's powerful favorites. Within Roman political institutions he had skillfully played the role of an emperor willing to accommodate the Senate. In his own household he had established himself on a plane above his fellow nobles with lavish displays of great extravagance. At the Circus and the theater he had shared the enthusiasm of the common people and won their hearts. He had acquired a political profile with a broad spectrum of sensible and necessary measures, ranging from expanding the equestrian order to improving Rome's water supply, projects to which virtually no objections could be raised. He had visited cities in Sicily, reorganized the regions on the eastern borders of the Empire, maintained friendly relations with rulers in the East, and planned extensive military actions against the Germanic tribes, which if successful would significantly strengthen his position as emperor. And he accomplished all this within twenty months, despite having been confined to his bed by illness perhaps for two of them.

It is safe to assume that some of the venerable old aristocrats of consular rank who set the tone in the Senate had begun to feel uneasy. Disquieting stories circulated: When Caligula was entertaining some royal guests—perhaps the kings named above—at a banquet in Rome, they began quarreling about the respective nobility of their ancestry. In response Caligula is said to have quoted Homer: "Let there be one king, one ruler!" (*Iliad* 2.204–5).

THREE

The Conflicts Escalate

THE CONSULARS' CONSPIRACY

"As for Gaius, he administered the Empire quite high-mindedly during the first and second years of his reign. By exercising moderation he made great advances in popularity both with the Romans themselves and with their subjects." With these words Josephus characterizes the period of Caligula's reign described up to this point (Jos. *Ant.* 18.256). The emperor stressed his respect for the Senate at the very beginning of 39 by some symbolic acts. When he assumed his second consulship on 1 January and resigned from it after only thirty days, he made a point of taking the oaths on the Rostra in the Forum as consuls normally did, behaving as one senator among others. His fellow consul, L. Apronius Caesianus, remained in office for six months, and Caligula was replaced as consul by Sanquinius Maximus, the city prefect. "During these and the following days," writes Cassius Dio in an abrupt end to his account of the start of the year 39, "many of the foremost men perished in fulfillment of sentences

Figure 4. Bust of Caligula. Copenhagen, Ny Carlsberg Glyptotek 637a (Inv. 2687). Photo: Jo Selsing.

of condemnation (for not a few of those who had been released from prison were punished for the very reasons that had led to their imprisonment by Tiberius), and many others of less prominence in gladiatorial combats. In fact, there was nothing but slaughter" (Dio 59.13.2–3).

What had happened? What had led suddenly to these events, which come as a complete surprise after the first two years of Caligula's rule? Why were so many men condemned, including numerous "leaders" (*prōtoi*), a term by which Dio usually means the highest category of senators, the *consulares* or former consuls? That some of them had been prosecuted for similar crimes under Tiberius and then released by Caligula suggests that they were convicted of the crime of *maiestas*. And since there are no indications at all of defamatory writings or verbal insults to the young emperor, the crime may have taken the most serious form of all, namely a conspiracy. Dio's reference to verdicts handed down by a court shows that the conspirators were found guilty in orderly trials in accordance with the law, presumably conducted by the Senate. But Dio, our sole source, who usually makes an effort to maintain chronological order, offers no information on the precise course of events and says not a word about whether there was actually a conspiracy or whether the condemned were just snared by denunciations. There are other passages in Book 59 of his *Roman History* in which Dio sometimes fails to discuss the motives behind actions, but here, at the decisive turning point of Caligula's reign, one has the impression that the author—or possibly the sources on which he based his account—intentionally passes over the background to these events in silence.

Other sources provide no further help. Suetonius just speaks in general terms about various conspiracies and provides a date only for the last one, which succeeded. Nor do Caligula's contemporaries Seneca and Philo show any interest in conspiracies against the emperor that might explain his later actions. Given the limited information provided by the sources, most modern biographies of Caligula shed no light on the early months of the year 39, the phase in which the relationship between emperor and aristocracy underwent a fundamental transformation.

A remark attributed to the later emperor Domitian runs: "Emperors' claims to have uncovered a conspiracy are not believed until they have been killed." If we assemble all the details in the various accounts, then this insight appears to apply to the present case. Dio goes on to mention that disagreements had arisen, clouding the relationship between Caligula and the people. At plays the crowd had chanted loud protests against informers, refusing to stop and demanding that they be handed over. This reveals that—for the first time under Caligula's rule—charges had been filed against a number of high-ranking aristocrats, including some who had their own supporters among the people, and that they were facing trial.

Soon afterward Caligula delivered a speech in the Senate (about which more will be said later), in response to which the Senators expressed their gratitude "that they had not perished like the others." We can infer from this that many more of them were considered guilty of the same crime. They voted to offer sacrifices to his philanthropy in the future. ("Philanthropy" [*philanthrōpia* in Greek, *clementia* in Latin] was the technical term for the mercy or benevolence that a ruler showed to someone who had opposed him.) And last they approved honors for the emperor including an "ovation," the "small" triumphal procession usually granted after military victories, "as if he had defeated some enemies" (Dio 59.16.9 and 11).

The evidence thus suggests a course of events as follows: In the period after Caligula resigned his consulate on 30 January, a conspiracy was uncovered in which many senatorial aristocrats had participated. The noteworthy feature of this conspiracy was that its leaders were neither old enemies of Germanicus's family nor former adherents of Gemellus, whom Caligula had prosecuted after his illness. We know this because it is expressly reported that some of them had been charged with similar crimes in the reign of Tiberius, that is, at a time when opposition to the family of Germanicus or support for Gemellus was more likely to lead to political advantage than to trouble. There is no indication that old scores were being settled, then. Furthermore it was the "leading men" of the aristocracy, that is to say consulars, who had initiated the conspiracy. In other words the leaders were men who, while they may have disliked the emperor's enthusiasm for Circus games and displays of extravagance and felt threatened by his plans for conquest, had received generally supportive and accommodating treatment at his hands.

The conspirators were charged and condemned in court proceedings. Was this Caligula's only reaction? In his account of the first half of 39 Dio mentions that some former senatorial office-holders stood trial for corruption. Several times, he reports, the senator Gnaeus Domitius Corbulo had drawn attention to deficiencies in the Roman road network that had arisen in Tiberius's time. Now with his help Caligula proceeded against all the men who had served as *curatores viarum* in the last few decades and received funds for road repairs but had not used them for the intended purpose. They—or the contractors whom they had hired—were required to pay the money back in full. Dio further mentions by name five senators who are supposed to have been victims of Caligula's persecution at that time. Investigation of these cases, however, provides no foundation for the claim that he had senators liquidated in great numbers.

Gaius Calvisius Sabinus, just returned from serving as governor of Pannonia, and his wife were accused of crimes and took their own lives, according to Dio. We learn nothing about the charges against the husband, but the wife was said to have inspected troops acting as camp guards in the province and to have watched soldiers as they drilled. As it happens, Tacitus in a different context records that the prosecution of the lady, at least, was entirely justified. She was accused of going about the camp dressed as a man and of committing adultery with an officer in the staff headquarters. The next man named is Titius Rufus, who committed suicide because he had said that the Senate thought differently than it spoke. This statement was undoubtedly correct, but for precisely that reason it is more likely that he was denounced by opportunistic colleagues rather than persecuted by the emperor. The praetor Junius Priscus was accused of various transgressions but the real reason for his trial, according to Dio, was his wealth. When it transpired after his death that he had not been particularly rich, Caligula is supposed to have remarked that Priscus had deceived him and could have remained alive. It is not possible to assess his case, since the charges against him are not named.

The case of Gnaeus Domitius Afer, a well-known orator of the time, is a different matter. He proposed an inscription to honor Caligula, but the emperor took offense instead. Reportedly Afer was able to save his own life only by resorting to servile flattery. He cannot have been in danger of death, however, since Dio writes that Afer had good connections to Caligula's freedman Callistus and was made a consul by the emperor soon afterwards—in the extremely volatile political atmosphere of the next conspiracy. Finally, Seneca is mentioned as someone who just barely escaped becoming a victim, because an outstanding speech he had delivered in the Senate aroused Caligula's anger. He was allegedly saved by the intervention of a woman close to the emperor, who told Caligula that he was suffering from an advanced case of consumption. This account does not seem very convincing either. Suetonius reports that Caligula made fun of Seneca's style and characterized it as "sand without lime"—an assessment that could have been made by a modern philologist as well. Seneca's oratory can thus hardly have been the grounds for his jeopardy.

On the whole then, beyond sentences for conspirators and the punishment of corrupt magistrates, there is no conclusive evidence that members of the aristocracy were prosecuted at that time. Caligula's reaction to the conspiracy of the consulars took an altogether different form. Although he did not resort to physical force, the effectiveness of his response left nothing to be desired.

THE MOMENT OF TRUTH

The emperor began by giving a speech in the Senate from which Cassius Dio provides extensive excerpts. In it he said things that the venerable assembly had never before heard, starting with a critical summary of how the members of the senatorial order had behaved over the past few decades. Caligula reproached the senators and people for the criticism they had heaped on his predecessor, Tiberius—in which he himself had previously taken part. "Thereupon," writes Cassius Dio, "he took up separately the case of each man who had lost his life, and tried to show, as people thought at least, that the senators had been responsible for the death of most of them, some by accusing them, others by testifying against them, and all by their votes of condemnation. The evidence of this, purporting to be derived from those very documents that he once declared he had burned, he caused to be read to them by the imperial freedmen." And he added, "If Tiberius really did do wrong, you ought not, by Jupiter, to have honored him while he lived, and then, after repeatedly saying and voting what you did, turn about now. But it was not Tiberius alone that you treated in a fickle manner; Sejanus also you first puffed up with conceit and spoiled, then put him to death. Therefore I, too, ought not to expect any decent treatment from you" (Dio 59.16.2–4).

This was a personal and direct attack on the assembled senators. Caligula presented a historical analysis of the behavior of the aristocracy under Tiberius, evidently supported by the advance work and documentary research of his freedmen. He confronted the senators with the fact that members of their own body, motivated by opportunistic desires to win the emperor's favor, had denounced other members. Furthermore, they themselves had pronounced the sentences of death against their colleagues. One can vividly imagine how the members of that august body felt as the freedmen on the imperial staff quoted from the records the statements they themselves had made during the trials for treason and then read the verdicts that the whole Senate had handed down. It must have been even worse, however, that in their presence—to their consternation, being senators—Caligula broached the subject of the opportunism and flattery that had characterized the Senate's communication with the emperor since the time of Augustus. By confronting the aristocrats in the Senate first with the honors they had bestowed on Tiberius and Sejanus and then with their completely contrary behavior after the two men's deaths—actions no one could deny—he exposed their behavior toward the emperor as consisting of hypocrisy, deception, and lies.

Yet there was still worse to come. Caligula conjured up an imaginary speech of Tiberius addressed to him: "In all this you have spoken well and truly. Therefore show no affection for any of them and spare none of them. For they all hate you, and they all pray for your death; and they will murder you if they can. Do not stop to consider, then, what acts of yours will please them, nor mind it if they talk, but look solely to your own pleasure and safety, since that has the most just claim. In this way you will suffer no harm and will at the same time enjoy all the greatest pleasures; you will also be honored by them, whether they wish it or not. If, however, you pursue the opposite course, it will profit you naught in reality; for, though in name you may win an empty reputation, you will gain no advantage, but will become the victim of plots and will perish ingloriously. For no man living is ruled of his own free will; on the contrary, only so long as a person is afraid does he pay court to the man who is stronger, but when he gains courage, he avenges himself on the man who is weaker" (Dio 59.16.5–7). Thereupon the emperor announced the resumption of the trials for treason, ordered his directives to be inscribed on a bronze stele, and left the Senate House.

Caligula had not only stripped the mask from the face of the aristocracy; he had also given a name to what lay behind it: their resentment of imperial rule, their hatred of the emperor, and their readiness to attack him whenever a favorable opportunity presented itself. No one could deny any of this, given the conspiracy against him that had just taken place. The truly appalling aspect of the speech, however, did not consist in what Caligula had said. There was no need to inform the senators of their own behavior. Every time they submissively voted some honor to the emperor, the senators knew what they were doing, and their latent willingness to conspire against him came as no surprise. What was unprecedented and shocking was that he had said it at all. By rebuking the Senate for the way it communicated with the emperor, Caligula had rendered it incapable of communication. The senators could not participate in his metacommunication about their ambiguous communication. The inequity of power prevented them from agreeing with him; they could not say, "Yes, we hate you and would gladly rid ourselves of you," a statement that by this point would probably have reflected reality. Instead they were powerless, helpless, speechless—and personally humiliated at the same time.

There was also a third factor. The mask on the emperors' part, their attempt to secure the aristocracy's acceptance by acting as though they were not autocrats at all—this mask too Caligula dropped. Augustus's art of lifelong playacting, which Caligula himself had copied in the past two years, was thus revealed as a lie, as dissembling and idle talk, that in the end only endangered the emperor's safety. Now he announced that he would dispense with the aristocracy's recognition of his position and predicted that aristocrats would remain servile nevertheless. This amounted to a declaration that the Augustan Principate was ended. Caligula had given the political paradox of the age, the contradictory combination of republic and monarchy, its real name, and declared himself for one side only, the monarchy.

How did the senators react? "For the moment," Dio writes, "their alarm and dejection prevented them from saying a word or transacting any business; but on the next day they associated again and bestowed lavish praise upon Gaius as a most sincere and pious ruler, for they felt very grateful to him that they had not perished like the others. Accordingly, they voted to offer annual sacrifices to his clemency,... on the anniversary of the day on which he had read his address" (Dio 59.16.9–10). In other words, they flattered him and so continued to address him in the very language he had exposed as hypocrisy the day before. They continued to show him honor, just as he had cynically predicted. It was their only chance—but it meant that they had taken their self-abasement toward the emperor and his power to the extreme.

With this speech Caligula had taken an irreversible step. To be sure, the consulars involved in the conspiracy had provided evidence of the ambiguity in relations between the aristocracy and the emperor. Their conspiracy had been secret, however, and the fact of the conspirators' enmity toward the emperor, revealed when the plot was exposed, could have been covered up in public by punishing the participants in the Senate. Now a new situation had arisen. Once the emperor had exposed the double-speak in communications between aristocrats and himself, every statement addressed to him by the Senate from then on had already been condemned in advance: It was duplicitous, and the emperor knew it. And the senators knew that the emperor knew that they knew that he knew. Conversely, the path was now blocked for every future attempt on the emperor's part to accommodate them: Everyone would have known that the emperor didn't mean what he was saying. And the emperor would have known that the senators knew that he also knew that they knew. In other words, Caligula caused the ambiguous form of communication to collapse, which up to that time had been the crucial means for avoiding the paradox of the simultaneous existence of a monarchy and a republic. The truth had been spoken, and that could not be undone.

How were they to go on from here? For the moment the aristocrats in the Senate had no choice but to carry on as before and thereby to abase themselves doubly—as flatterers who had been exposed but continued their flattery nevertheless. As for Caligula, he did not drop the matter after this one speech; rather he used the new situation to humiliate the aristocrats and make them look ridiculous.

By the time of Augustus and Tiberius the continuation of traditional friendships among aristocrats had produced a situation in which all senators and the highest-ranking knights were officially "friends" of the emperor, whatever their actual personal relationships with him. Mornings they visited him at home; in the evening they were his guests or invited him to banquets; they left bequests to him in their wills, to gain his favor. Thus ambiguity prevailed here, too. Although Caligula had now torn down the facade of friendship, he continued to impose the traditional modes of behavior on the aristocracy, and its members were incapable of expressing their enmity to the emperor openly, because all the power was on his side. It is reported, for example, that he addressed many people as "father," "grandfather," "mother," and "grandmother," that is, by names that conveyed a close and affectionate relationship to them, in order to compel them to make him "voluntary" payments and to bequeath him money. Through a resolution in the Senate, he ordered that all those still alive who had included Tiberius in their wills must now name him instead. Similarly, when his daughter was born a short time later he pointed out the expenses he would incur as a father and demanded "gifts" for her education and dowry. Once again the aristocrats had to pay up or cause their own downfall by demonstrating publicly that they were no friends of the emperor. Philo reports that Caligula made gifts of money to force people to give him far higher amounts in return. Particularly distinguished members of the senatorial order were harmed in other ways "under the guise of friendship." They were required to pay vast sums for his travels and entertainment when he visited them; some spent their entire fortunes on a single dinner or even went into debt. "And so some came to the point of deprecating the favors bestowed by him" (Phil. *Leg.* 345).

That was Caligula's second response to the conspiracy by his consular "friends." After having himself unmasked the pretense of friendship between emperor and aristocracy, for a cynical humiliation he made use of the fact that nonetheless no other alternative possibility for their conduct was available. He treated his aristocratic "friends"—that is, the aristocracy as a whole—as if their friendship toward him were actually sincere. Since no one could deny it, given their behavior, he was able to damage them financially as well. They were helpless, and Caligula is said to have made no secret of how much enjoyment that gave him.

Similarly, he compelled senators to pay large amounts of money to sponsor games in Rome. Presumably after the reintroduction of popular elections, he reinstated the old custom of choosing two praetors by lot to present gladiatorial games. Further, he put up his own gladiators for sale and attended the auction in person; his presence had the effect of driving up the prices, since bidders felt obligated to do him a favor in this way. Suetonius provides an account of how Caligula could indulge his sense of humor at senators' expense during such auctions: "A well-known incident is that of Aponius Saturninus; he fell asleep on one of the benches, and as the auctioneer was warned by Gaius not to overlook the Praetorian gentleman who kept nodding to him, the bidding was not stopped until thirteen gladiators were knocked down to the unconscious sleeper at nine million sesterces" (Suet. *Cal.* 38.4).

He did not stop there. Dio reports how Caligula invited Incitatus ("Hotspur"), his favorite race horse, to dinner, fed him barley corn made of gold, toasted him with golden goblets, and planned to make him a consul. The meaning of this last gesture, perhaps the emperor's most notorious, which seems to make no sense, can be inferred from the parallel account by Suetonius, who reports that in addition to a marble stall, a manger made of ivory, and purple blankets, Caligula gave his horse a palace, a staff of servants, and a dinner service so that the guests received in his name could be entertained as grandly as possible. Lastly Suetonius also mentions that the emperor planned to appoint the horse to the consulship.

There is no way now to know whether everyone in Rome got this joke. Nor can we tell whether Suetonius understood it later or—as seems more likely—failed to understand it on purpose, since he makes use of it to present the emperor as insane. There can be no doubt, however, about who in Rome would have gotten the point at the start of 39. The households of the senators—their houses, servants, and dinner services—represented a central manifestation of their social status and were in part an item of ruinous competition that was served up at wasteful banquets, and laws were passed from time to time to restrict extravagance. Achieving the consulship remained the most important goal of an aristocrat's career. To equip the emperor's horse with a sumptuous household and to destine it for the consulship satirized the main aim of aristocrats' lives and laid it open to ridicule. Caligula placed his horse on the same level as the highest-ranking members of society—and by implication equated them with a horse.

Besides symbolically devaluing the Roman consulars, Caligula's designation of Incitatus as a consul sent a further message:
The emperor can appoint anyone he likes to the consulship;
consulars are consulars by the grace of the emperor. In fact there
was no alternative to the system that awarded status to members
of the upper class in Rome according to their standing in the
Senate, a form of ranking that had been in place for centuries.
But if an individual possessed the minimum requirements—
being in the third freeborn generation and of unblemished
character—his position within this hierarchy was now decided
by the emperor. In fact the emperor could even grant the rights
of free birth, *ingenuitas,* and so make knights even of men born
as slaves. Caligula's joke about his horse not only made the consulars look ridiculous, but also expressed a truth about Roman
society that members of the highest rank found extremely dis-
agreeable: The position of every one of them depended on the
emperor's goodwill.

All this, then, was Caligula's response to the unexpected
attempt on his life by the consulars: Instead of issuing orders for
heads to roll indiscriminately, he took aim at their positions
in the Senate, in relationships of patronage, and in the hierarchy
of their society—confronting them with the unpleasant reality
of the Empire and with their own duplicitous behavior in dealing with their lack of real power. He forced them to humiliate
themselves. He dishonored them by cynicism and symbolic acts.
He left them to their impotence and absurdity.

Was this radical shift of behavior on the emperor's part
"appropriate"? The extent to which it was or was not cannot be
determined with certainty, since the sources are silent on the
motive for the conspiracy that preceded the shift and on its
scope and object. That Caligula was still following a policy of

demonstrative cooperation with the Senate at the start of the year, however, suggests that something extreme had occurred. In any case one feature of Caligula's response is clear. Striking at the core of the senatorial aristocracy's position in society had the desired effect. Conflict between emperor and aristocracy had suddenly erupted, and now the groundwork had been laid for its escalation. The only question was what would be the next opportunity for venting the stored-up hatred. The wait was not long, and the occasion came with two measures intended to stabilize the emperor's position.

In the summer of the year 39 Caligula remarried. He was again attempting to clarify the dynastic situation by having an heir. The bride, Milonia Caesonia, is said to have been neither young nor particularly beautiful, but she had already proved her fertility by having borne three children—and she was well along in a pregnancy. After the baby was born, Caligula referred to Caesonia as his wife and acknowledged the daughter, who was named Julia Drusilla, as his own. The order of events indicates that this time the emperor waited to marry until a child had actually been born, a child who represented the purpose of the union.

There was a not inconsiderable side effect to Caligula's now having legitimate offspring, however. His sisters, Agrippina and Livilla, and their descendants were apparently to be permanently removed from possible succession to the throne. Yet Agrippina in particular had demonstrated her ambitions for the succession a year and a half earlier (and would do so again in later years). When her marriage to Gnaeus Domitius Ahenobarbus, a very aristocratic but ailing older man, had produced a son, the later emperor Nero, she had asked Caligula to name the child. Her hopes that the emperor would choose "Gaius" and thereby grant him a special place in the dynasty were in vain, however.

Caligula instead suggested the name of their uncle, Claudius, a member of the imperial family whom no one took seriously at that time. Now, with the birth of Caligula's daughter, Agrippina's chance to be the mother of an emperor was tending toward zero. She now shared the situation of Aemilius Lepidus, who had lost a once promising position after the death of Drusilla.

The build-up for a military campaign against hostile tribes in Germania led to a further and lasting consequence. As later events would show, Caligula, given the state of his relations with the aristocracy, was preparing this expedition with great urgency in the months following the conspiracy. Since 29, the Roman commander on the upper Rhine had been the senator Gnaeus Cornelius Lentulus Gaetulicus. He had survived Sejanus's fall despite their having had a close connection, though there were rumors that Tiberius had issued a barely veiled threat to him at that time. Gaetulicus had written to the emperor, according to Tacitus's account, that he would remain loyal, but if the emperor named a successor the commander would regard it as a certain death sentence. Gaetulicus proposed a kind of bargain, whereby the emperor would remain in charge of the rest of the Empire, but he would keep his province. At the time he got away with it. He had achieved great popularity with his soldiers, though clearly at the expense of discipline. The attacks by tribes in the region, Caligula's official reason for his campaign, were probably a consequence of Gaetulicus's long command; at the very least he had to accept responsibility for them. The way Caligula had proceeded against corrupt magistrates in Rome and the prospect that the emperor would soon arrive in the Rhineland in person must have prompted in the senator well-founded fears about his future fate.

As a result, shortly before the emperor's twenty-seventh birthday, a crisis began to brew that would eclipse everything that had gone before. Events in the following weeks show that around the middle of the year a new conspiracy formed, which would take on dramatic dimensions.

THE GREAT CONSPIRACY
AND THE EXPEDITION TO THE NORTH

At the core of the conspiracy were Lepidus, the emperor's most important senatorial confidant, and Gaetulicus, the commander in upper Germania. Other participants included members of Caligula's immediate family: his two sisters, Agrippina and Livilla, to whom in the previous two years the emperor had awarded the highest honors. Agrippina had entered into an affair with Lepidus "out of her lust after power," as Tacitus puts it (*Ann.* 14.2.2). A large number of senators were also privy to the plot, among them both consuls—the highest magistrates of the Roman polity—who had taken office on 1 July. The conspirators could thus count on military backing in the Empire, on broad support among the aristocracy, on the most important officeholders in Rome, and on some of the emperor's closest relatives—meaning that they also had a presumptive future emperor and empress handy. Caligula himself had confirmed the man's suitability for rule by including him in his own plans for the succession, and the woman provided the prestige of the current emperor as a "dowry," so to speak. Agrippina's son Nero even offered a prospective successor in the next generation. These were probably the best conditions for a conspiracy in the whole history of the Roman Empire. All that remained to do was to assassinate Caligula.

But things did not go as planned. The sources do not reveal who betrayed the plot to the emperor, and its full scope does not appear to have been clear immediately. Evidently only Gaetulicus and senatorial circles in Rome fell under suspicion at first. Caligula's response was swift and effective. In the early days of September he removed the two consuls from office and ordered his minions to break their fasces, the bundle of rods that symbolized their office and the power connected with it. One of the consuls committed suicide. Caligula replaced them with Domitius Afer, mentioned above, who was close to the emperor's freedman Callistus, and Aulus Didius Gallus, a senator from an obscure family who was known to be ambitious. Presumably at the same time, the emperor withdrew from the Senate's hold the last military unit that had remained formally under its control, the legion in the province of Africa, and replaced its commander. Next Caligula traveled to the town of Mevania in Umbria. He had given no sign that he planned a longer journey, but in a surprise move he pushed on from there as swiftly as possible toward Germania. The pace of the march is said to have been so fast that the Praetorian Guard had to use pack animals to carry its standards, and orders were given to cities and towns along their route to wet the roads, to keep the dust down. Traveling in Caligula's retinue were Lepidus, Agrippina, and Livilla, who had not yet come under suspicion.

An attempt to reconstruct in detail what happened in the following weeks and months runs into a number of difficulties. For one thing, what is true of ancient reports about Caligula in general applies in even greater measure to the great conspiracy of mid-39 and his march north to Germania: The central facts of the case are reported explicitly and in a reliable way, since they appear in contexts only indirectly related to Caligula himself.

Where Caligula's own actions are concerned, however, ancient historians try to present them as incoherent and senseless, occasionally entangling themselves in blatant contradictions in the process. Cassius Dio, for example, reports that Caligula ordered the consuls' *fasces* to be taken from them and broken because they had failed to celebrate his birthday properly—a remark that at least establishes the date securely. Suetonius claims that Caligula's sudden expedition to Germania grew out of a plan to add to the Germanic bodyguard that served him as it had his predecessors on the throne. Yet in the same breath he writes that for this purpose legions and auxiliary troops had been gathered from all over the Empire, new recruits had been raised, and provisions collected "on an unheard-of scale." Dio writes that the threat posed by Germanic peoples was merely a pretext; in reality the emperor was in financial difficulties and organized the military campaign in order to plunder wealthy Gaul. Yet he mentions only a few sentences later that the troops assembled for the purpose numbered between 200,000 and 250,000, and that the money raised in Gaul was used mainly to pay for this army. In addition both authors' accounts of how the conspiracy was put down and how the campaign proceeded in Germania portray Caligula's behavior as absurd and grotesque—thereby demonstrating above all, once again, that this was not what happened.

Modern scholars have debated the subject at length. While the state of the sources means that some questions cannot be answered with certainty, nevertheless it is possible to trace in outline a course of events that appears plausible. As in other distorted accounts of the emperor, we can deduce a basic framework from the overall pattern of events, the mention of details in parallel sources that have no reason to seem suspect, and, last but not least, information that Suetonius and Dio included even though it contradicted the impression they wished to create, probably because the facts were too well known to be suppressed.

To begin with, Caligula's abrupt departure for the North clearly accomplished his primary purpose. Gaetulicus was taken by surprise and had no time to prepare his legions for an open uprising against the emperor. He was executed, presumably in Mainz, and replaced by Servius Sulpicius Galba, a capable general who was to become emperor himself briefly a few decades later. The full scope of the conspiracy apparently came to light only at this point, perhaps because Gaetulicus betrayed the others in an attempt to save his own skin. Lepidus, Agrippina, and Livilla were found guilty as accessories to the plot to assassinate the emperor; Lepidus was executed, and the two sisters were banished to the Pontine Islands. Caligula forced Agrippina to take an urn with the ashes of her lover Lepidus back to Rome, carrying it against her body for the whole journey. The emperor divulged documents in their own hands revealing their share in planning the conspiracy. He also distributed money to the soldiers as a reward for their continued loyalty to him, and sent the three swords with which the plotters meant to murder him to Rome, where they were placed in the Temple of Mars Ultor ("Mars the Avenger") as dedicatory offerings. Last, he informed the Senate in a letter about the assassination he had narrowly escaped and forbade the senators to vote honors for any of his relatives in the future. The dating of these events can be reconstructed from a fragmentary inscription of the priestly college known as the Arval Brethren. On 27 October 39 they performed a sacrifice to offer thanks that "the nefarious plans of Gnaeus Lentulus Gaetulicus against Gaius Germanicus were detected." It can thus be inferred that reports of the general's disloyalty had reached Rome by then, but the guilt of Lepidus and the emperor's sisters had not yet been made public.

What went on in the young emperor's mind in these days is not reported, but it is not difficult to imagine. This time it was not high-ranking senators in Rome who had plotted to take his life, as at the beginning of the year—but members of his innermost circle. Even his own sisters, the people who were undoubtedly closest to him personally, had joined in a conspiracy to assassinate him. The comparatively mild treatment they received probably points to the close relationship that once existed among the siblings. In view of what had occurred, Romans would certainly not have considered it an overreaction if both of them had been put to death—a step, incidentally, that would have prevented Nero from ever becoming emperor. In whom could the emperor place any trust from then on? That was the overriding question of the moment. Relatives—his uncle Claudius, for example—were out of the question, as his prohibition of new forms of honor for any members of the imperial family made abundantly clear. Could he trust senators? That was unthinkable after what had taken place earlier in the year.

In Rome, too, at the center of the Empire, the dramatic events led to a general sense of uncertainty. Legal proceedings were taken against individuals who could be shown to have had conspiratorial contacts with Caligula's sisters or the men who had been executed. In addition to the consuls, who had already been removed from office, several aediles and praetors had to resign from office and stand trial. Many who had not taken part in the plot must have felt uneasy as well. The disclosure of the conspiracy appears to have launched a wave of denunciations, not unlike what had occurred under Tiberius. Thus, for example, we know from the biography of the later emperor Vespasian, who was a praetor at the time, that ambitious men of modest origins took advantage of the situation to display their loyalty to the emperor. This group included Vespasian himself, who made a motion in the Senate to leave the corpses of the conspirators executed in Rome unburied—a proposal not in the best of taste, but indicative of the atmosphere in that period.

The Senate voted an ovation for the emperor, just as it had done after the first conspiracy at the start of the year, and sent a legation to inform him of their action and to demonstrate their support. To lead the group, they chose none other than Claudius, the man who possessed the greatest dynastic prestige after the emperor himself since the banishment of Agrippina and Livilla, and who would in fact later succeed Caligula on the throne. The emperor was outraged. The Senate had violated his express prohibition against honoring members of his family when they put Claudius in charge of the mission. Caligula also seems to have feared further plots. He sent most of the legation back to Rome before it even reached him, because he believed their real purpose was to spy on him and wished to prevent them from having any contact with members of his personal or military retinue. Only a few chosen delegates were permitted to continue on and meet with him, including Claudius, whom Caligula allegedly humiliated and threatened after the mission arrived.

Given this volatile situation of fear and mutual distrust, Caligula must have decided first and foremost to stabilize the military, since in the end his position of power rested on the army. His sudden departure for Germania had upset the original plans for war. It was now the beginning of November, and the season alone made a military campaign on the right bank of the Rhine unfeasible. In addition, the Rhine legions were in such a miserable state that they would not have been capable of carrying out a rapid strike.

Caligula's first measures were thus aimed at reorganizing the troops there. A large number of centurions—key officers in the Roman military forces—were discharged on the grounds of age and poor physical condition, and the customary payments on retirement were reduced. Several commanders of forces redeployed to Germany from other provinces of the Empire received dishonorable discharges because they had arrived on the scene too late. Evidently they were suspected of having held back intentionally, waiting to see if Gaetulicus's uprising would succeed. Galba, on the other hand, who had not stinted with his active support, received a special commendation. As the new supreme commander he was charged with making the army of the upper Rhine fit for action again. He refused soldiers' requests for leave, and re-accustomed them to military discipline by constant maneuvers and forced marches in which he took part himself. Suetonius cites a saying that circulated among the troops and reflected the new conditions: "Soldier, learn to play the soldier; 'tis Galba, not Gaetulicus" (*Galba* 6.2). On the lower Rhine near Cologne and Xanten, where four further legions were stationed, another military reorganization appears to have taken place about the same time. There Lucius Apronius was relieved of his command and replaced with Publius Gabinius Secundus. The families of Apronius and Gaetulicus were connected, and Apronius had been responsible for several catastrophic defeats in battles against Frisian tribes.

In his *Life of Galba*, Suetonius reports that during that autumn the new governor repelled "barbarians" who had advanced even into Gaul, and in the *Life of Vespasian* he writes that the later emperor, then a praetor, proposed in the Senate among other things that special games be held to mark the emperor's victory over the tribes in Germania. Dio's account states that the emperor had himself acclaimed *imperator* a number of times. Thus it is apparent that several military engagements occurred in the fall of the year 39 and ended successfully for the Romans. In his *Life of Gaius Caligula,* however, the same Suetonius relates some bizarre stories depicting the military actions carried out under the emperor's command as pure farce. He reports, for example, that Caligula gave orders to some men from his Germanic bodyguard to cross the Rhine and hide there. Then he arranged for a report to be brought to him after breakfast with a great to-do that the enemy had arrived, and he rushed off with some friends and cavalrymen from the Praetorian Guard to a nearby wood, where they chopped down trees and dressed them up to look like trophies. In the evening the emperor returned by torchlight and rebuked the men who had stayed behind, calling them cowards; to the participants in his "victory," however, he awarded a new kind of military decoration. Since Suetonius himself included passages in his biographies of other emperors about very serious military engagements on the upper Rhine, which were at least partly successful despite the condition of the troops, the story about the game of hide-and-seek can easily be recognized as a military exercise in which the emperor personally took part. Suetonius has taken the event out of context and distorted it.

Tacitus elsewhere briefly reports the vast scale of the preparations, but no extensive military action could be carried out before winter began. Caligula therefore left the front along the Rhine and spent the winter in Lyon, capital of the province of Gallia Lugdunensis, which at that time was also the site of the sole imperial mint for coining precious metals. Clearly tax assessments were calculated here in order to finance the huge war effort, as is reflected in Dio's claim that the emperor had the tax rolls of Gaul brought to him and gave instructions for the richest inhabitants to be executed. It is doubtful, however, that he actually selected this particular way to raise revenue, for at the same time the emperor put his sisters' entire sumptuous household effects up for auction, including their slaves and even freedmen. Since the auction was a great success, Caligula afterwards ordered much of the valuable inventory accumulated in other households of the imperial family during the reigns of Augustus and Tiberius to be sent from Rome and auctioned off as well. The shipments were reportedly so large that the government had to seize private vehicles; the transportation of grain to Rome was affected and there was a shortage of bread. Dio states that Caligula conducted the auctions personally, and that "the finest and most precious heirlooms of the monarchy" came under the hammer (Dio 59.21.5).

Dio writes that people attending the auction were forced to buy, but this, again, seems quite unlikely. The wealthy residents of the cities in Gaul probably sought to furnish their houses with luxurious objects like the aristocracy in Rome, and "the objects of the old court" (Suet. *Cal.* 39.1) would no doubt have seemed extremely attractive to them. Dio says that in auctioning off the objects the emperor was simultaneously selling "the reputation" attached to them (Dio 59.21.6). Both the interest of the Gallic nobility in acquiring prestige through some connection with the emperor and the group's economic power are documented in an anecdote from Suetonius: A rich man in the province wanted to attend one of Caligula's banquets and had paid the servants a bribe of 200,000 sesterces to smuggle him in—a sum, it should be recalled, equal to half the minimum amount required for a Roman to qualify for membership in the equestrian order. When the emperor heard of it, he arranged for the man to purchase some small object for the price of 200,000 sesterces at auction the next day and sent a message that he might now attend the emperor's banquet at his personal invitation. Yet Caligula did not just take in money at Lyon; he also spent it on a grand scale. He sponsored splendid festivities befitting an emperor visiting a provincial city, including theatrical performances, games, and a contest for orators in both Greek and Latin. In addition he granted Roman citizenship to the inhabitants of the town of Vienna (modern Vienne).

Meanwhile the atmosphere in Rome was less festive. The aristocracy feared that the emperor would take further measures, as became evident on 1 January 40, when the absent Caligula began his third consulate. His co-consul had died shortly before. The praetors and tribunes of the people, whose task it would have been to call the Senate into session in the consuls' absence, did not dare to proceed, fearing to give the impression that they were acting in the place of the emperor, without instructions from him. All political business of the Senate thus halted until 12 January, when a message arrived from Caligula that he was resigning from the consulate. Thereupon the senators in a body climbed the steps to the Capitol, offered sacrifices in the temple there, and performed the act of *proskynēsis,* prostrating themselves before an empty throne. Following that, they assembled in the Curia without any official summons and spent the day giving speeches praising Caligula and offering prayers on his behalf, "for since they had no love for him nor any wish that he should survive, they went to greater lengths in simulating both these feelings, as if hoping in this way to disguise their real sentiments" (Dio 59.24.6). When the two new consuls had assumed office, it was decided *inter alia* henceforth to celebrate the birthdays of Tiberius and of Drusilla with the same ceremonies as that of Augustus, and in consequence of a letter from Caligula statues of Drusilla and himself were erected and dedicated.

In Gaul an important military decision was made at about this time, to abandon the campaign in Germania in favor of an attempt to conquer Britain. Given the state of the sources we can only speculate about what was behind this move, as about other military events of that time. In all likelihood there were protracted discussions; considering the more or less complete failure of Roman policy in Germania since Varus's catastrophic defeat in the Teutoburg Forest in A.D. 9, disagreement would hardly have been surprising. The emperor was probably looking for a quick military victory as well, since the situation in Rome was extremely tense after exposure of the conspiracy. The spur for the change of plans seems to have been a dispute over the succession to the throne of Cynobellinus (Cymbeline), king of the Britons. Furthermore, the Romans would have regarded a successful conquest of the distant island as a highly prestigious achievement. Since Julius Caesar's expeditions in 55 and 54 B.C., no other Roman general had set foot in the country; and two years after the death of Caligula, Claudius would demonstrate that a conquest of Britain was entirely possible and a suitable enterprise for stabilizing the emperor's position.

Once again the sources are scarce and unclear. On the one hand, the British king's son Adminius is said to have left the island with a small force and surrendered to Caligula, whereupon the emperor wrote a boastful letter to the Senate implying that the prince had handed over the whole island to him. On the other hand, it is also reported that when Caligula reached the ocean, presumably the English Channel, he drew up his soldiers in battle formation and set to sea himself in a warship, but only briefly. Then he returned and gave the legions an order to collect shells on the beach. As a symbol of victory they constructed a tall light; the soldiers received the amount of 400 sesterces each, and Caligula concluded the maneuver by announcing, "Go your way happy; go your way rich" (Suet. *Cal.* 46).

Perhaps the most plausible explanation of the events was suggested by the English scholar Dacre Balsdon. He bases it on the reports about Claudius's expedition to Britain in 43. At that time the Roman legions mutinied, declaring that the island lay outside the bounds of the *oikoumenē,* the civilized world, and refusing to cross the Channel to Britain. Only after several weeks could they be persuaded to embark for a campaign. Something similar could have happened at the start of 40. In that case the order to collect seashells and the bonus payment should be interpreted as the emperor ridiculing the cowardice of mutinous troops, who had assembled at the edge of the sea but refused to fight.

There is no knowing what actually happened in any detail, but Suetonius, after describing the scene at the water's edge, adds an odd incident further suggestive of a mutiny: Before leaving the province Caligula was said to have intended to order a massacre of two legions. After he had been dissuaded from this extremely dangerous plan, he wanted at least to decimate them, that is, to use the traditional method to punish cowardice in the Roman army, in which every tenth man in a legion that had been cowardly in the face of the enemy was killed, regardless of how he had behaved himself. The plan failed, Suetonius says, because the legionaries realized what was afoot and rushed to get their weapons. Thereupon the emperor hastily fled from the assembly.

Suetonius accounts for Caligula's inclination to punish the men by mentioning that the legions involved were the same ones that had mutinied after the death of Augustus in A.D. 14. At that time his father, Germanicus, had been their commander and Caligula, then a small child, had been present in the camp himself. It is obvious how little credence should be given to this account: The usual period of military service for an ordinary legionary was twenty years; centurions could serve longer. After twenty-six years, in other words, hardly any of the participants in the original mutiny would have been left in the legions. In any case, carrying out a punishment at that critical juncture would have been a completely senseless act on the emperor's part. It corresponds precisely, however, to the portrait of Caligula that Suetonius consistently seeks to draw.

It seems, then, that the campaign against the Britons may have failed because of a mutiny in which legions I and XX took part; both had refused to fight in A.D. 14 and had now joined Caligula's forces from their original station on the Rhine. This conclusion is supported by Anthony Barrett's analysis of circumstances within Britain. In his view, the general conditions would definitely have favored an aspiring conqueror at that time, if Caligula and his troops had only mounted an attack.

Looking at the enormous expense and effort Caligula's military campaigns required, Tacitus characterizes them as ludicrous and attributes their failure to the emperor's capricious nature. In fact Caligula achieved no conquests worth mentioning. An impartial assessment must record, however, that he quelled a revolt by the governor of one of the militarily most important provinces in the Empire and corrected deficiencies in the troops along the Rhine that had gone unaddressed for years. Much evidence suggests that Caligula created the conditions in which Claudius was able to conquer Britain three years later. It should also be kept in mind that all long-term planning for military campaigns had to be tossed overboard once the great conspiracy was uncovered, and that the expeditions all were attempted while the situation in Rome was highly uncertain.

Last, there are various indications that the abrupt end of the mission and Caligula's swift return were prompted by new threats against him from aristocratic circles. In connection with events at the English Channel, Dio mentions that Caligula showed "no little vexation at his commanders who won some slight success" (Dio 59.21.3). This remark points to conflicts between the emperor and the commanding officers of the military, who all came from the senatorial order. Such tensions can hardly have arisen if the officers' successes were in carrying out the emperor's orders. Furthermore, the close of military actions coincided with a great intensification of the emperor's hostility toward the aristocracy as a whole, for which the sources provide no other convincing explanation. On his way back to Rome Caligula encountered another delegation from the Senate asking him to hurry, which suggests there was an urgent need for him to take action in the capital. Thereupon, the account runs, Caligula shouted at the top of his voice, "I will come; I will come, and this will be with me," tapping the hilt of the sword at his side. At the same time he proclaimed in an edict that "he was returning, but only to those who desired his presence, the equestrian order and the people, for to the Senate he would never more be fellow citizen nor *princeps*" (Suet. *Cal.* 49.1). He also gave up plans to celebrate a triumph, and forbade any senators to come out to meet him en route; in other words, he announced that he would have no further social contact with his fellow aristocrats.

RESHAPING THE EMPEROR'S ROLE

The conspiracy of Agrippina, Livilla, and Lepidus had presented Caligula with the same threat in extreme form that had always been present under the rule of his imperial predecessors and that his successors on the throne would face a number of times: The very people who made up the emperor's closest circle could endanger his safety. Precisely because they were close to the ruler, because they could influence his decisions and allow or deny others access to him, they had power that could also be turned against the emperor himself. This gave rise to a paradoxical situation in which the emperor had to be most mistrustful of the people he trusted most. The problem was exacerbated in the case of a close family relationship or high social standing. Already under the first two emperors this danger had had consequences for the selection of their staff, which had been called into service for precarious power-political tasks. This is seen not only in the equestrian rank of the Praetorian prefects and the governor of Egypt but also on occasion by the employing of freedmen (former slaves) of the emperor's household in highly confidential posts. These last were particularly well suited for their positions, since in contrast to individuals of high rank or members of the imperial family, freedmen owed everything to the emperor. Without him they were nothing. While they might become a threat to him in court intrigues, they could never aspire to replace him. Caligula was the first Roman emperor systematically to exploit the advantage this group offered.

After Lepidus was executed and the emperor's sisters banished, we hear nothing more of Roman aristocrats who acquired influence and wealth as members of Caligula's inner circle or through close personal ties to him. When he appeared in public in the city he was of course still accompanied by a retinue of high-ranking "friends" from the aristocracy, including Claudius, but after the expedition to Gaul the circle of Caligula's closest confidants and aides consisted of quite different people.

One of the central figures in this group was the freedman Gaius Julius Callistus. Nothing is known about his background. His daughter Nymphidia, mother of the later Praetorian prefect Nymphidius Sabinus under Nero, is said to have been Caligula's mistress as a young woman; that may be how the two men encountered one another. Callistus appears to have played a role in the detection of the great conspiracy. In this extremely perilous situation it was he who persuaded the emperor to give the consulate to Domitius Afer. In the aftermath, according to Josephus, the fear he inspired in people and his great wealth enabled him to achieve enormous influence and power "no less than a tyrant's" (Jos. *Ant.* 19.64). Another close confidant, probably also descended from slaves, was Protogenes. He "assisted the emperor in all his harshest measures" (Dio 59.26.1) and is supposed to have carried around two catalogues labeled "Sword" and "Dagger." They apparently recorded the behavior of the six hundred members of the Senate (too large a number to keep track of in one's head) and the intended punishment for each, should the necessity arise—something that caused the secretary to become a terrifying figure for the aristocracy. Another important role was played by the Egyptian slave Helicon, originally a gift for Tiberius, who worked his way up to become Caligula's valet. Philo reports that Helicon was always at Caligula's side, doing gymnastic exercises with him, and accompanying him to the baths. Since he remained near the emperor when he ate or slept, Helicon seems to have served some of the functions of a bodyguard as well. He advised Caligula on decisions, controlled access to him, and used his position to his own advantage by taking bribes—or at least that is what Philo claims, who had bad experiences with him.

Another member of the new inner circle around Caligula was the empress Caesonia, who had borne him a daughter and with whom he was passionately in love, according to the sources. She, too, was considered to be an influential adviser and apparently remained in Rome during Caligula's expedition to the North, acting as his stand-in. Finally, by virtue of their positions a significant role fell to the two Praetorian prefects. Cassius Dio names both, in addition to Callistus and Caesonia, as the emperor's most important confidants.

All the above-named people acquired political prominence only after the great conspiracy and Caligula's sojourn in Gaul. After his experiences in 39 the emperor consciously embarked on a new path in exercising rule. He removed all the aristocrats from his inner circle and thereby also from the political nerve center of the Roman Empire. The background for this measure was the emperor's need for personal security, and it was directed against Rome's traditional political institutions, the Senate and magistrates. At the same time, some people outside the center gained importance in political operations although they had no connection at all with the old institutions. Thus, for example, after the events on the shore of the English Channel Caligula authorized his procurators—financial agents—to confiscate funds as they saw fit to pay for his triumph in Rome (the one that was later called off). Officers of the Praetorian Guard were authorized to collect taxes and unpaid tribute as well. In other words, the emperor used the structures available in his household and in the military to administer political tasks for which they had previously had no responsibility.

The fundamental changes were not limited to the ways in which central rule was organized, for Caligula also dealt with a problem no emperor before him had addressed: the social rank of the emperor himself. Up to that point he had followed his predecessors' example in allowing the Senate to confer extraordinary honors on him that, although they had raised the emperors far above the other members of the aristocracy, had at the same time remained permanently linked to the traditional aristocratic ranking. In its turn this system of rank was based on the various classes of senatorial office (consular, Praetorian, etc.) and thus ultimately on the structures of the old Republican magistracy, that is, on a political order that had not merely not foreseen the possibility of a monarchy, but had excluded it on principle. Thus at the heart of the matter was a paradoxical process: Precisely by undermining the traditional ranking system in order to place himself at the top of it, the emperor provided proof both of its continuing validity and of his having no independent claim to monarchical rank. When he allowed the Senate to award him distinctions, he confirmed that he needed the old Republican institution in order to manifest his social standing. By accepting honors he emphasized that he lacked them on his own.

Caligula is the only Roman emperor of whom it is reported that he grasped this very paradox and made an issue of it himself. Cassius Dio, writing about the first delegation from the Senate after the great conspiracy had been uncovered, reports that Caligula's response was to prohibit the Senate from passing any furthers honors to him: "For he did not for a moment wish it to appear that anything that brought him honor was in the power of the senators, since that would imply that they were his superiors and could grant him favors as if he were their inferior. For this reason he frequently found fault with various honors conferred upon him, on the ground that they did not increase his splendor but rather destroyed his power" (Dio 59.23.3–4).

But what would a monarchical position of honor look like once it surpassed the limits of the old Republican order of ranking, which was the only such order existing in Rome, and had been in place for centuries? The coming weeks and months would reveal Caligula's plans on the subject. His first priority was display of material splendor, since after the old political ranking this was the second way Romans showed off their social status. Caligula had begun to exceed conventional limits of luxury some time before, but in this respect, too, he altered his behavior after the sojourn in Gaul. The auction of the household goods of his predecessors can be interpreted not only as a source of income but also as a conscious break with elements that had previously served to represent the emperor's social position. Thus fundamental changes in the way the emperor's role was shaped were taking place here as well. Yet the decisive question remained: What, for the emperor, would replace traditional manifestations of rank? It was true not just of ancient Rome but of all premodern aristocratic societies that each individual's social status became a reality only when it achieved visibility in public.

The circle of people closest to Caligula during his stay in Gaul was not entirely free of aristocrats; it was free only of Roman aristocrats. According to Cassius Dio, among the emperor's entourage were the rulers of two client kingdoms in the Hellenic East whom he had placed on their thrones in 37, Julius Agrippa of Judaea and Antiochus IV of Commagene. Another such ruler, Ptolemy of Mauretania, seems to have gone to Lyon as well, but was then condemned to death by Caligula under circumstances that are unclear but may have had something to do with political changes in the province of Africa. These kings embodied another tradition, of sole rule established over the course of centuries in the Hellenic empires of the East. Such kings were independent of urban political structures and urban aristocrats; they headed political administrations that had grown out of their own household staffs and answered to the monarch alone. The rank of the aristocrats and nobles around such kings was linked to a court hierarchy at whose apex the king stood unchallenged. And, last but not least: Since the third century B.C. it had become customary in the East for the kings, who occupied a position so far above everyone else, to be worshiped as godlike beings, with cultic rites. In describing the turn of the year 39 / 40 during Caligula's reign, Cassius Dio mentions particular concern in Rome when the news arrived "that King Agrippa and King Antiochus were with him, like two tyrant-trainers" (Dio 59.24.1). What looked liked tyranny from the perspective of Roman senators can be described in other words: Caligula was starting to alter the paradoxical and dangerous role he had played up to that point as an emperor in a republic, and to create an openly monarchical system.

TRIUMPHANTLY CROSSING THE SEA

Caligula's swift return journey to Italy ended before the gates of Rome. He was at the shrine of the Arval Brethren outside the city walls near the end of May in 40, and possibly about the same time he received on the first occasion the embassy of Alexandrian Jews, led by Philo, in the gardens of his mother, Agrippina, which likewise lay outside Rome. Two circumstances above all probably kept Caligula from entering the capital immediately. Events over the previous few months must have made the situation in Rome extremely volatile; for that reason alone, concern for the emperor's safety would have ruled out an official entry amid large crowds of people. Then again, a return from Germania without any ceremony at all would have looked like an admission of defeat. On the other hand, the emperor had expressly forbidden the Senate to provide any formal welcome and other honors, so that a triumphal procession of the usual kind was out of the question. In its place Caligula chose a new way to stage his return, one without precedent in Rome. It alluded to the events of the northern campaigns, surpassed all previous triumphs, and was so imposing that even Suetonius includes it among the few deeds of the "good" ruler Caligula. To achieve this, the emperor proceeded to his luxurious villas near Puteoli in Campania and prepared to demonstrate his power as he had been prevented from doing at the English Channel: by triumphantly crossing the sea.

A bridge of ships a little more than three miles long was constructed in the Gulf of Baiae between Puteoli and Bauli (near Misenum). It consisted of a double row of cargo ships assembled from many places, with earth piled on top of them to make a road as solid as the Via Appia. At various intervals the road was widened to make space for resting places and shelters with running fresh water. When the entire structure was finished, Caligula put on the breastplate of the most famous ruler of the Greek world, Alexander the Great, which had been taken from his grave; over it he wore a purple cloak of the kind used by Greek military commanders, with gold decorations and jewels from India. Wearing a sword at his side, carrying a shield, and with a crown of oak leaves on his head, he sacrificed to the gods, first of all to Poseidon, the god of the sea, and Invidia, the goddess of envy, so that he himself would not be a target for envy. Then he rode onto the bridge from Bauli, accompanied by troops of cavalry and infantry. On reaching the other side he stormed into the town of Puteoli like a general bent on conquering it.

The following day the troops rested, as if after a victory, and then the return march began. This time Caligula wore a tunic embroidered with gold and drove a chariot pulled by the most famous race horses of the day. Behind him followed a long column with articles of plunder that had obviously been brought back from the North, as well as a Parthian prince who was being kept in Rome at that time as a hostage. Next came a procession of chariots carrying his *cohors amicorum,* the "friends" who made up the aristocratic retinue of a Roman general, wearing cloaks of blossoms, followed by the Praetorian Guard, the army, and further supporters who had decorated their clothing however they saw fit. The entire train proceeded to the center of the bridge, where a stage had been erected on top of the ships. There the emperor gave a speech: "First he extolled himself as an undertaker of great enterprises, and then he praised the soldiers as men who had undergone great hardships and perils, mentioning in particular this achievement of theirs in crossing the sea on foot. For this he gave them money" (Dio 59.17.7). After this speech a festive banquet was held on the bridge and on ships anchored nearby for the rest of the day and the following night, during which bonfires illuminated the bridge, the bay, and the surrounding mountains like a stage set.

At the end of the celebration "he hurled many of his companions off the bridge into the sea and sank many of the others by sailing about and attacking them in boats equipped with beaks. Some perished, but the majority, though drunk, managed to save themselves" (Dio 59.17.9–10). The emperor boasted that he had turned the sea into dry land and the night into day, mocking the Persian rulers Darius and Xerxes (who had crossed the Bosporus and the Hellespont on bridges of ships in the years 513 and 480 B.C.) because he himself had crossed a much wider expanse of water.

Caligula's horseback ride over the sea made a deep impression, as the ancient sources attest. According to Seneca, while the emperor was amusing himself with the resources of the Empire, the dearth of available ships was endangering grain supplies to Rome. Both Seneca and Josephus use the event to illustrate the emperor's insanity. Suetonius mentions contemporary interpretations that come closer to the heart of the matter. These averred that Caligula wanted to outdo Xerxes (as Dio also reports) and at the same time to inspire fear in the Germanic tribes and Britons, whose borders he was threatening. The reason given by Suetonius himself reflects the web of anecdotes that was spun around the event in the next hundred years. When Suetonius was a child he had heard court gossip from his own grandfather that Tiberius, concerned about his grandson Gemellus's prospects for rule, had consulted the astrologer Thrasyllus. Thrasyllus told him that Caligula had about as much chance of becoming emperor as of crossing the Gulf of Baiae on horseback. The story does not quite add up, since Caligula was already emperor by then and had been for some time, but it does exemplify how incredible the deed was. According to Dio, the crossing should be seen as Caligula's disdain for a triumph: The emperor would have regarded being pulled by horses across dry land as too ordinary, and hence had wanted to cross the sea.

In fact, in addition to its demonstration of unlimited power, the staging of the crossing contains several symbolic references. The connection with events on the coast of the Channel is obvious: The emperor showed that in Italy, unlike the distant North, he was not dependent on the goodwill of his troops and the cooperation of his senatorial generals; at home he had the power to lead his soldiers on foot even across the sea. The ride from Bauli to Puteoli was thus a symbolic demonstration of the emperor's potential power to conquer Britain. The return journey, with the emperor driving a chariot followed by trophies and spoils, was modeled on a triumphal procession, and the ensuing feast on the bridge was in a sense designed to outshine the triumph he did not have in Rome (which he himself had rejected). The ironic praise for the bravery of his "friends" and soldiers and the dunking that followed also point clearly to the events of the spring. They designated who was really responsible for the fiasco at the Channel and simultaneously expressed Caligula's bent for mocking and humiliating those who resisted his assertions of power.

The events at the Gulf of Baiae are revealing in yet another respect, however. They manifested imperial grandeur by means of ceremonies that broke through the conventional Roman semiotic system for assigning social rank. Traditionally the achievement and display of social honor was connected to holding political offices in the Roman polity and functioning as a magistrate of the city: It was office that conferred honor on the man who held it. Accordingly a Roman aristocrat achieved the highest possible distinction if the political institution of the Senate voted him a triumphal procession, which wended its way through the city with great splendor before the assembled citizenry of Rome and reached its ceremonial culmination on the Capitoline Hill. Hence when Caligula demonstrated his imperial superiority to all others in a new manner and with great publicity, it is noteworthy that he did so for the first time outside the city of Rome and independently of the Senate and the Roman polity. This corresponded precisely to his announcement that he would not permit the Senate to vote him any more honors, and to his perceiving the paradoxical situation that arose if honors for an emperor were granted by the Senate and aristocracy. The triumphal ride across the sea thus represented Caligula's first attempt, through new ceremonial practices, to make real his position as a monarch who stood above the aristocracy. But were these practices in fact new?

Caligula deployed a semiotic system that comprised Roman elements, first and foremost the triumphal procession, along with elements borrowed from ancient non-Roman monarchies. The Persian kings Xerxes and Darius served as points of reference in that their achievements were being outdone, along with Alexander the Great, with whom Caligula symbolically identified by wearing his breastplate. Thus the ceremonial actions on the bridge at Puteoli drew on the ways in which Persian and Hellenistic rulers displayed their royal status, and, despite the inclusion of some Roman elements, represented an extreme break from Roman traditions. Since the earliest days, since the legendary times when kings had been driven out of Rome, monarchy had been despised there as a degenerate form of government, as tyranny. It is safe to assume that the new inner circle Caligula formed after the great conspiracy, the "tyrant-trainers" as people in Rome were calling them, played a part in designing the new arrangements for presenting the emperor's status. Those at whose expense this innovation had to be effected will hardly have admitted to themselves that thereby he was seeking a way out of the paradoxical combination of autarchy and republic that had already been bought with a great deal of blood. They will have suspected, though, that Puteoli was only the beginning.

FOUR

Five Months of Monarchy

SUBJUGATING THE ARISTOCRACY

On his twenty-eighth birthday, 31 August A.D. 40, Caligula reentered Rome after a year's absence and was greeted with an ovation. We can glean only indirectly what had occurred in the city during the preceding months, after the emperor's open threats. Those days must have resembled the end of Tiberius's reign. In his time, denunciations, accusations, trials in the Senate, torture, and executions had been the order of the day. Now the question was: How would the young emperor deal with the senators in Rome, after everything that had happened in the previous year? He had staged a public demonstration of his role as sovereign ruler, independent of Republic and aristocracy, by riding horseback over the sea. How would he now impose his authority in the venerable capital of the Empire, where the Senate and the aristocracy were inescapably present? The fears of the Roman nobility are reflected in the claim (reported by several sources) that after his return Caligula planned to eliminate the entire

Figure 5. Bust of Caligula. Copenhagen, Ny Carlsberg Glyptotek 637 (Inv. 1453).

Senate or the most distinguished men of both the senatorial and the equestrian orders.

The emperor did indeed rely on fear and violence, but he employed them in his own characteristic manner. Whereas Tiberius had stood helplessly by as the aristocracy destroyed itself in the trials for *maiestas*, Caligula promoted the disintegration of Rome's noble society and used it to his own advantage. He let the aristocracy do itself in. The events are reflected in the accounts of the sources, which claim several times that baseless executions of senators and high-ranking knights at the emperor's instigation were becoming the order of the day. Strangely, however, these reports mention only a few victims by name, and investigation of the individual cases exposes the tendentiousness of such a sweeping judgment.

Seneca reports that after a long argument with the Stoic philosopher Julius Canus the emperor ordered his execution, for which the philosopher mockingly offered his thanks. The condemned man spent the ten days until his death perfectly calmly, playing board games and discussing philosophical questions. There is some evidence that that the emperor did not order his execution on a whim, however, for a later source notes that Caligula had accused Canus of being an accessory to a conspiracy against him. Tiberius had attempted to rein in the Senate's zeal for *maiestas* trials by introducing a requirement that ten days must elapse between sentencing and execution. The circumstances therefore suggest that Canus was formally accused of conspiracy and sentenced to death by the Senate.

There is less clarity in the case of Julius Graecinus's death, which also appears to fall in this period. Seneca claims that Caligula killed him because he was too good a man to be of use to a tyrant. Graecinus was the father of Agricola, Tacitus's father-in-law. In Tacitus's biography of Agricola he is depicted as an example of steadfast conduct in the face of the emperor, so lacking in Rome at that time. A noted orator and philosopher himself, Graecinus had refused to prosecute Marcus Silanus and was for that reason eliminated by Caligula, as Tacitus reports. Silanus had died by his own hand near the start of 38, however, while according to Tacitus's account Agricola was born on 13 June of Caligula's third consulship, in 40 (and apparently at a time when his father was still alive). Whatever the reason for Graecinus's death, then, it cannot have been a steadfast refusal to prosecute Silanus.

The only reported instance of courage and strength of character in the autumn of 40 that stands up to closer examination involves not a senator, but a freedwoman, to whose case Caligula responded with pity rather than cruelty. According to Cassius Dio, a high-ranking senator named Pomponius was accused of conspiracy by a friend named Timidius; in Josephus's version of the incident, the charge was *maiestas* and Timidius an enemy of the accused. (At that time, of course, it was difficult to tell one from the other.) Timidius named as his witness Quintilia, an exceptionally beautiful actress with whom Pomponius was having a love affair. Cassius Chaerea, an officer of the Praetorian Guard, tortured Quintilia so badly that afterwards she was permanently disfigured, but she neither denounced her lover (if he was innocent) nor betrayed him (if he was not). When she was brought before the emperor he was touched by her appearance and impressed by her behavior. He released Pomponius and gave Quintilia a present of 800,000 sesterces for her steadfastness.

Indeed not only were the senators denouncing one another in order to voice their ostensible fear for the emperor's safety and thereby to procure personal advantage for themselves. Some sought to strike anew, to transform their pent-up hatred for the emperor into action. A third conspiracy of aristocrats against Caligula took shape, although in the end it was no more successful than the first two. According to Seneca, one night in the lamplight of a festive gathering attended by ladies and other senators, Caligula had three men beaten with whips, tortured, and brutally killed for his "amusement." They were Sextus Papinius, whose father had been consul; Betilienus Bassus, an imperial quaestor and the son of an imperial procurator; and an unnamed senator. Before their execution they were gagged so that they could not utter rebukes. Centurions went to the houses of the victims' fathers that same night and killed them as well.

From the parallel account of Cassius Dio it emerges that these executions were not arbitrary sadism on the emperor's part but rather swift measures to defeat the new conspiracy. Dio mentions that a certain Anicius Cerialis (whom he mistakenly considers a victim) was involved. This same man is mentioned by Tacitus in a different context, where there is no reason to suspect unreliability; there the author says that during the reign of Nero he attracted attention through his exceptional opportunism: After the Pisonian conspiracy of 65 he brought forward in the Senate the motion that a temple to the divine Nero should be erected at public expense. Not long afterward he was charged with crimes himself and committed suicide; few people pitied him, Tacitus reports, since they remembered that he had once betrayed a conspiracy against Caligula. Seneca's account, written shortly after Caligula's death, is thus revealed once again as tendentious and denunciatory, because he leaves out the conspiracy to which the emperor was reacting. Furthermore, in his effort to paint the aristocracy as the emperor's helpless victims, Seneca suppresses a senator's role in betraying the conspirators, a betrayal still recalled in Rome a quarter of a century later.

An episode that appears credible precisely because it is reported in aristocratic sources documents the disintegration prevailing within the senatorial order after the exposure of a third conspiracy, and how Caligula made use of it. After Papinius and Bassus had been executed, Caligula called the Senate into session and granted the remaining members impunity, adding that there were only a few toward whom he still bore ill will. Naturally this only increased the level of fear and uncertainty among those present. During a later session of the Senate that Caligula did not attend, Protogenes, the emperor's confidant, who kept the books for him on the conduct of the aristocracy, entered the building. As the senators were greeting him and shaking his hand, he gave the senator Scribonius Proculus a sharp look and asked him, "Do you, too, greet me, when you hate the emperor so?" (Dio 59.26.2).

During the reigns of Augustus and Tiberius a person accused of hostility toward the emperor had usually met a swift demise, since either he was prosecuted by opportunistic fellow senators and sentenced to death by the Senate as a whole or he committed suicide. In this instance the senators fell to work immediately without waiting for formal procedures; according to Dio they surrounded their colleague in the Senate House itself and tore him to pieces. Suetonius reports that Proculus was stabbed with pens and ripped apart; his limbs and entrails were then dragged through the streets and piled up before the emperor. Suetonius claims that Caligula incited certain individuals to this savagery, without mentioning that they were senators; he does not deny, however, that all the others joined in. In any case, the scene manifests the senators' fear of reprisals and at the same time their utter lack of scruples, up to and including murder, each man prepared to save his own skin at the others' expense. Certainly the emperor had a part in the staging of the affair. He exploited aristocrats' willingness to tear one another to pieces—in this instance literally—for his own purposes, without having to get his hands dirty.

"Gaius showed pleasure" at the death of Scribonius Proculus, Dio reports, and declared that he had become reconciled with the senators. In response "they voted various festivals and also decreed that the emperor should sit on a high platform even in the very Senate House to prevent any one from approaching him, and should have a military guard even there" (Dio 59.26.3). The fact that the emperor needed a guard in the Senate (a measure to which Augustus had also had recourse in precarious situations, and which the Senate had once offered to Tiberius) shows that the dominant mood after what was now the third conspiracy within a year and a half was in fact anything but conciliatory. At the same time the senators' decree documented once more the absurdity of the paradoxical communication between the emperor and the aristocracy. In one and the same resolution the Senate revealed both its concern for the emperor's safety and the fact that the threat to his life stemmed from its own members, from the same people who had voted the resolution.

The military guard now posted in the Senate was not the sole consequence of the conspiracy. Behind the facade of reconciliation the emperor increased his pressure on the aristocracy, creating even more fear. Josephus reports that Caligula permitted slaves to bring charges against their masters at that time, and to his satisfaction they made copious use of the privilege. If one remembers that a high-ranking aristocrat might have several hundred slaves in his palace in Rome and that some masters were anything but humane in the exercise of their authority (which included the right to kill), it is not hard to imagine how alarmed the nobility must have felt. Now they were not safe from betrayal or denunciation even in their own homes. Any unguarded conversation could be dangerous, and their own servants could turn them in.

It must be said that this measure was not Caligula's invention, as Josephus suggests. In Tiberius's reign Sejanus had ordered slaves and freedmen to be tortured as a way of obtaining evidence against their masters, and two years later Claudius too used the denunciation of slaves and freedmen against their masters as a means of revealing the background of the first conspiracy against him. Now, during Caligula's reign, Claudius became a victim of the tactic. A slave of his named Polydeuces denounced him, but without success. Josephus writes that Caligula appeared at Claudius's trial, hoping (in vain) that his uncle would be sentenced to death. It is an open question whether this is true, but the report does indicate that the emperor had no direct influence on the outcome of trials: Once again he left it to the senators to condemn one another.

But that was not all. Suetonius reports, without giving a date, that the emperor sought to increase his revenues not only by establishing certain new taxes, but also by opening a brothel on the Palatine Hill and making Roman matrons, that is, married women, and freeborn boys available in rooms whose elegant furnishings betokened the dignity of the place. Then he sent his nomenclators to all the markets and public halls to invite young and old to come and satisfy their desires. Allegedly customers could borrow money at interest, and the emperor's clerks wrote their names down openly, because they were contributing to his revenues. Once again we have a bizarre story intended to demonstrate Caligula's "madness" but self-contradictory. If someone is short of money, he doesn't furnish spaces lavishly and then lend money at interest. More likely the story reveals the harshest measure the emperor used to demoralize the aristocracy.

What actually happened can be inferred from Cassius Dio's account of the end of A.D. 40 (where he says nothing about a brothel). He mentions that the occupants of the newly furnished rooms near the imperial palace were "the wives of the foremost men as well as the children of the most aristocratic families," and he might have added that this location meant they could easily be seized by the Praetorian soldiers guarding the emperor. Dio writes that Caligula forced them to live there at exorbitant cost, but notes at the same time: "Some of those who thus contributed to his need did so willingly, but others very much against their will, lest they should be thought to be vexed" (Dio 59.28.9). Supposedly the plebeians were pleased by the aristocrats' discomfiture and about the "gold and silver" that the emperor collected from his tenants.

Suetonius, then, suppresses the fact that the occupants of these quarters were the wives and children of the *prōtoi* (the word Dio uses), meaning the consulars; he reverses the direction of the payments and turns the apartments into a brothel. If we leave aside this last and set both reports in the context of the now frequently reported manner and habit in which the emperor exploited the aristocracy's code of behavior, then it becomes clear what was going on. Remember that relationships between the emperor and the aristocracy continued to be expressed in the old ceremonies of friendship, morning receptions, evening banquets, reciprocal support in financial matters, and testamentary bequests. In this process it had become necessary for imperial nomenclators to keep records of the emperor's "friends," because there were so many he could no longer keep track of them himself. After the consulars conspired against him in early 39, Caligula had cynically exposed the ambiguity of these forms of communication by reproaching them for their enmity and hatred for him, but then demanding payments of money from individuals on the basis of their friendship with him, which no one could disavow. The highest form of imperial favor was the privilege to live as *familiares* on the Palatine in the palace buildings, a dispensation known from reports about other emperors, such as Agrippa in the reign of Augustus, or later Titus Vinius, Cornelius Laco, and Marcianus Icelus under Galba.

So once again Caligula took aristocrats' protestations of friendship at face value and showed extraordinary favor to the leading consulars. After their conspiracy was exposed they had shown concern for his safety by murdering Scribonius Proculus and voting him a military bodyguard in the Senate. Now he responded by allowing their wives and children to live on the Palatine Hill, where they could enjoy the greatest possible proximity to the emperor, a distinction in which all of them took so much satisfaction. Simultaneously his nomenclators, who kept the lists of the emperor's friends and the favors they did for one another, visited the former consuls and asked them for a gift in return.

In actual fact, of course, this meant that the emperor was holding the family members of the Senate leadership hostage on the Palatine under the eye of his Praetorian Guard, while at the same time extorting payments of gold and silver from the senators, forcing them to pay "voluntarily," as Dio notes expressly, since one can describe paradoxical circumstances only in paradoxical language. This was Caligula's response to the third attempt to murder him. He had put aristocrats in their place again and continued to humiliate them with jokes. At a solemn banquet he suddenly burst out laughing; the two consuls, who were reclining on the couches next to him, politely inquired what had amused him so. "What do you suppose," he replied, "except that at a single nod of mine both of you could have your throats cut on the spot?" (Suet. *Cal.* 32.3). We have already observed in Suetonius's style a kind of montage technique (and will encounter it again in further examples), in which he takes Caligula's cynical jokes literally, thereby distorting their meaning and presenting his behavior as aberrant. Caligula in these days may have had even a further joke, particularly about the new building on the Palatine, the wives and children living there, and the profits resulting from them that he had provided for himself: "I now have a brothel on the Palatine."

If we adopt Seneca's moral standards (and if we bear in mind that the aristocracy itself—and Seneca in the opinion of the aristocracy—was utterly depraved according to these standards), then we can agree with his drastic conclusion: Caligula was the emperor who showed how "far supreme vice could go, when combined with supreme power" (Sen. *Ad Helv.* 10.4). The Roman aristocracy was finished, its resistance broken.

DISHONORING THE ARISTOCRACY

The steps Caligula took against the aristocracy after returning from the North were not limited to furthering their self-destructive tendencies, encouraging slaves to denounce their masters, and interning consulars' wives and children on the Palatine. He also set about destroying the foundation of every aristocracy: its honor. Following the earlier consulars' conspiracy he had mocked how hollow the old aristocratic conceptions of honor were under a changed form of government by granting awards to his horse Incitatus. Now, after two further conspiracies, he shifted from symbolic actions to concrete ones. Josephus and Suetonius report that the emperor abolished reserved seating for senators and knights at the theater. As a result there were pushing and shoving, and even fights, before performances began, and the highest-ranking members of society were forced to compete with commoners for a place. The seating order was left to chance. The emperor is said to have been amused by it all. His primary motive was certainly to annoy the aristocracy, but at the same time the resulting thoroughly mixed order of seating demonstrated that differences in rank were observed only when the emperor stood behind them; if he failed to support them, they were obsolete.

As the emperor allowed traditional social distinctions to be abolished by society itself, he also set about strategically dishonoring individuals among the leading members of the aristocracy. His uncle Claudius, who enjoyed particular distinction because of their close relationship, received much the same treatment as Silanus had earlier. Caligula decreed that of all the former consuls Claudius should always be the last to vote in the Senate. Because rank coincided with the order of voting, he was thus permanently demoted to the lowest place among them. But the emperor's main targets were now the remaining members of the higher ranks of old Republican aristocracy, the *nobilitas,* who played a leading role in the group of *consulares.* He ordered that the statues of famous men from the Republican era, which Augustus had moved to the Campus Martius, be taken down, and announced that in the future he alone would decide in whose honor statues and portraits could be displayed. Living members of distinguished old families were prohibited from using certain emblems of an ancestor's fame to which they had traditionally been entitled. A Torquatus was forbidden to wear his torque, a Cincinnatus could not wear his lock of hair, and a descendant of Pompey lost the right to add "the Great" to his name.

In the last case Caligula's proceeding can be traced in some detail. Suetonius describes these insults without naming a year, making them seem arbitrary, but they can in fact be dated with relative precision. Pompey's descendant, a great-grandson on his mother's side of the famous Pompeius Magnus, is still listed with the unshortened form of his name in an inscription from the start of 40. Thus the prohibition of the cognomen belongs among the measures ordered by the emperor after his return to Rome. Secondly, Dio reports the reason Caligula gave for withdrawing the honor: He remarked that "it would be dangerous for anyone to be called Magnus ['the Great']" (Dio 60.5.9).

This statement could also have come from a modern social historian. "Noble birth still ... was perilous," writes Ronald Syme in his famous study of the early Empire. Every emperor had a "rational distrust" of the old *nobilitas,* whose very existence challenged his claim to exercise rule alone, for "even if the *nobilis* forgot his ancestors and his name, the emperor could not." This Pompey's later fate took a predictable course. The emperor Claudius restored his cognomen and even chose him as a son-in-law. But then the combination of distinguished ancestry and membership in the emperor's inner circle proved to be too much of a good thing. Falling victim to an intrigue of the empress Messalina in 47, he lost his life "because of his family and his relationship to the emperor" (Dio 61[60].29.6a). Caligula turned out to be right in the end. But he was not a social historian, and Pompey cannot have had any interest in abstract insights. Caligula's remark represents a cynical insult added to the injury. Not only did he devalue Pompey as a potential rival; he openly alluded to the dangerous rivalry between him and members of highly distinguished families. He thus justified the dishonor inflicted on Pompey with the need to protect him from the ruler—from himself.

As Pompey's case shows, the most painful humiliations for the aristocracy undoubtedly occurred in personal contact with the emperor. Philo reports that even though everyone suffered from Caligula's actions, people still continued to flatter him. Among the guests at the emperor's last banquet in early 41 was Quintus Pomponius Secundus, one of the sitting consuls and a half brother of the empress Caesonia. According to Cassius Dio, Secundus sat at the emperor's feet—like a slave—during the meal and "kept bending over continually to shower kisses upon them" (Dio 59.29.5). Suetonius recounts that when the emperor dined in the evening sometimes a few senators who had occupied the highest offices would stand at the head or foot of his couch dressed in short linen tunics: that is, comporting themselves in the manner of his personal slaves.

Thus the forms of debasement suffered in personal contact with the emperor began with voluntary, submissive, individual acts; when Caligula did not discourage these, everyone else was obliged to imitate them. This was not a new phenomenon. Tacitus used strong language to characterize aristocrats' opportunistic behavior under Augustus and Tiberius and, as we have seen, they acted no differently under Caligula even before the autumn of 40. Now, however, the emperor began to demand self-abasing behavior from them. Dio writes that to most senators he offered his hand or foot to kiss but did not kiss them in return—an act that would have symbolized equality in rank. In one hate-filled passage, Seneca describes an incident in which a consular wished to thank Caligula for saving his life; clearly he had been denounced, and he may have been the lover of Quintilia. The emperor held out his left foot to be kissed, and this man, who had held the highest offices in Rome, prostrated himself and kissed the emperor's foot in the presence of the leaders of the Senate. Caligula further subverted the traditions of the social hierarchy by offering the honor of his kiss in public to favorites whose official rank was far below the senators', such as the well-known actor Mnester.

The reaction of aristocrats to their ceremonial degradation is illustrated by Dio's report that those senators who were granted the exceptional honor of a kiss from the emperor thanked him in speeches in the Senate. The submissiveness continued, in other words. But Caligula went further in using his contacts with the aristocracy to humiliate specific individuals. All the sources mention his rhetorical talent and his quick wit, and we have noted his fondness for cynical jokes.

A sense of the horror aroused by Caligula's presence among senators forced into submissive behavior has been preserved in various accounts: "Amid the multitude of his other vices," writes Seneca, Gaius Caesar "had a bent for insult" and "was moved by the strange desire to brand every one with some stigma." Seneca immediately gave him a taste of his own medicine by describing his appearance: "Such was the ugliness of his pale face bespeaking his madness, such the wildness of his eyes lurking beneath the brow of an old hag, such the hideousness of his bald head with its sprinkling of beggarly hairs. And he had, besides, a neck overgrown with bristles, spindle shanks, and enormous feet" (Sen. *De Const. Sap.* 18.1). According to Suetonius, Caligula's face "was naturally forbidding and ugly," but "he purposely made it even more savage, practicing all kinds of terrible and fearsome expressions before a mirror" (Suet. *Cal.* 50.1).

It cannot be verified whether Caligula's feet were in fact enormous or whether he used a mirror to practice making horrible faces. Here again, remember that the behavior described as illustrating the emperor's character can belong only to the time after he returned to Rome in the autumn of 40. Josephus and Dio's accounts show that up to the time of the consulars' conspiracy he had treated the aristocracy courteously, and after the great conspiracy he had spent a year away from Rome. The fears that he inspired in senators from then on, and his consistent efforts to humiliate them, thus formed part of a conscious new strategy. Much of it, especially the insults directed at individuals, should probably be ascribed to the emperor's desire to take personal revenge and should be taken as his response both to the events of the previous year and to the most recent conspiracy. But Caligula's remarks on the emperor's paradoxical position of honor within the senatorial class show that his goal went even further: His aim was to destroy the aristocratic hierarchy as such and expose it to ridicule.

THE EMPEROR AS "GOD"

Lucius Vitellius, Suetonius reports, "was the first to begin to worship Gaius Caesar as a god; for on his return from Syria he did not presume to approach the emperor except with veiled head, turning himself about and then prostrating himself" (Suet. *Vit.* 2.5). The father of the later emperor had presumably been replaced as governor of Syria at the beginning of the year and then must have feared for his life. Dio provides more details. In order to save his life, Vitellius dressed as a man of lower rank than he actually was, threw himself at the emperor's feet, addressed him with many divine names, prayed to him, and finally vowed that he would offer sacrifices to him. In other words, in Caligula's presence Vitellius performed a ritual combining an element of Roman cultic practice (veiling the head) with the custom known in the Hellenic world and the East of prostrating oneself before a divine ruler (*proskynēsis*). He started a trend.

After Caligula released Pomponius, Dio relates, the senators praised him "partly out of fear and partly with sincerity," some calling him a demigod (Greek *hērōs*) and others a god (Dio 59.26.3–5). They didn't stop there. In accord with a decree of the Senate a temple was built to the emperor; he was to be worshiped there as divine. A college of priests was founded to take charge of the emperor's worship. "The richest citizens used all their influence to secure the priesthoods of his cult and bid high for the honor" (Suet. *Cal.* 22.3). Dio writes that "these honors paid to him as a god came not only from the multitude, accustomed at all times to flattering somebody, but from those also who stood in high repute" (Dio 59.27.3). What had happened to the senators of Rome? Had fear driven them insane? Not at all. Their behavior was less surprising than it may appear at first glance.

The heaven of the ancients was not nearly as distant as that of Christianity, the religion beginning to spread from the East at that time. In the myths handed down in the ancient world, the gods were not above appearing on earth from time to time, for instance for the purpose of pursuing attractive mortal women. Similarly, from the fourth century B.C. on it was possible to designate persons who possessed power or wealth far in excess of human norms as "heroes" or gods and to venerate them accordingly. In Hellenistic times this led to the founding of cults for individual kings and their dynasties. Roman senators who had conquered the Greek East in the era of the Republic had direct knowledge of this custom, since they had been objects of the same kind of veneration there themselves. Finally, Roman emperors and members of their families were worshiped as gods in the eastern cities of the Empire and not long afterwards in the western provinces as well. Caligula had experienced this himself as a child when he accompanied his parents to the East.

In Rome itself the situation was somewhat more complicated. Julius Caesar had been offered various divine honors by the Senate before he was assassinated. He was designated "Jupiter Julius," and plans were made for a temple dedicated to him and his clemency; Marcus Antonius was chosen to serve as his priest. In the time of Augustus poets such as Ovid, Horace, and Propertius often addressed the *princeps* as a god, and in Tiberius's reign various senators attempted to gain recognition by attributing a divine aura to him. Thus it is reported that the emperor's activities were called "sacred occupations," that offerings were made to images of the emperor and Sejanus, or that some senators prostrated themselves before him.

The idea of divinity seems to have been not entirely without appeal for recipients of the honor. Alexander the Great and other Hellenistic kings had sometimes appeared attired as various deities, and Roman senators were not unfamiliar with performances of this kind: In a triumph, the highest honor achievable, a victorious Roman general appeared dressed to resemble Jupiter, the supreme god of the Roman polity. Wearing a tunic embroidered with palm trees and red make-up on his face, he carried a scepter; all three features were typical attributes of the god. It is reported of Octavian, the later Augustus, that during the triumvirate he gave a party that became known as the "banquet of the twelve gods," at which he appeared costumed as Apollo and the guests also came dressed as divinities. His rival Antonius did not lag behind. He allowed himself to be honored in the eastern parts of the Empire as the "new Dionysus" and appeared with the corresponding costume and paraphernalia.

When he assumed the position of *princeps* in 27 B.C., however, Augustus altered his behavior in this respect, as he did in many others. When the civil wars ended, he refused divine honors, since they would have run directly counter to his aim of being accepted as sole ruler by reviving Republican forms and honoring the senatorial order as equals. As emperor he seems to have insisted that throughout the Empire he should not be honored in a cult of his own, but only in conjunction with the capital city, so that temples were dedicated to *Roma et Augustus*. Tiberius followed a similar policy. He rejected the idea of such honors for himself and was criticized by the Senate for it. He permitted others in their place, however, granting to the cities in the province of Asia in 23, for instance, the right to erect one temple to him, his mother, Livia, and the Senate. The attempts of some senators to flatter him obsequiously apparently repelled him; every time he left the Senate House, he supposedly exclaimed, "These men! How ready they are for slavery!" (Tac. *Ann.* 3.65.3).

There had been, then, no shortage of attempts to venerate emperors as divine even before Caligula's time. These did not entail belief that the emperors were superhuman; rather they formed part of the ambiguous communication that had become requisite in imperial Rome. The first two emperors had tried to block this development because they feared correctly—as could be seen in Caesar's case—that the more honors the aristocracy awarded them, the lower their acceptance sank among those very aristocrats. The Senate itself was venerated as "sacred" or as a "divine assembly," in some cities in the eastern part of the Empire, after all, so that worship of the emperor as a god would clearly detract from the "divinity" of its members. This did not prevent some senators from pushing for veneration of the emperor all the same, and their colleagues could hardly voice any objection.

Now the question was how Caligula would react to the veneration of his person. Clearly he was in a different position from his predecessors in that he did not need to weigh acceptance by the aristocracy in his decision. That was a thing of the past, since open enmity now reigned. The offer of worship belonged to the mode of ambiguous communication the senators still practiced, both out of fear and because they lacked an alternative; it had nothing to do with whether they actually accepted his position as emperor. Caligula was clearly aware of all this: He himself was the one who had pulled back the curtain a year and a half earlier, after the consulars' conspiracy, and exposed their manner of communicating with him for what it was: obsequiousness and insincere flattery. So how did he now respond to veneration of himself as a god by the "divine assembly"?

Caligula was the first emperor who *permitted* the aristocracy in Rome to venerate him as divine. Suetonius provides a description of the temple that was erected "to his own godhead" (*numen*). "In this temple was a life-sized statue of the emperor in gold, which was dressed each day in clothing such as he wore himself," and the animals sacrificed to him were "were flamingoes, peacocks, black grouse, guinea hens, and pheasants, offered day by day each after its own kind" (Suet. *Cal.* 22.3). But Caligula not only allowed the senators to pray to the golden statue of him; he allowed himself to be worshipped as a god by them. He "built out a part of the palace as far as the Forum, and making the Temple of Castor and Pollux its vestibule, he often took his place between the divine brethren, and exhibited himself there to be worshiped by those who presented themselves; and some hailed him as Jupiter Latiaris" (Suet. *Cal.* 22.2). The terms Suetonius uses suggest that Caligula turned the customary morning *salutatio*, when the senators and others greeted the emperor at home, into veneration of himself as a god. In addition it is reported that he appeared not only as Jupiter, but also costumed as a great variety of other ancient gods, both male and female: as Hercules, as one of the Dioscuri, as Dionysus, Hermes, Apollo, Ares, Neptune, Mercury, or Venus. At times he appeared shaved, at other times with a golden beard; he would appear with or without a wig, depending on which god he was portraying. And the senators of Rome worshiped him. What did that mean? Had *the emperor* now gone mad? In this case, too—as in the case of the senators—the answer is clearly no.

The German scholar Hugo Willrich has conjectured that by allowing himself to be worshiped as a god Caligula intended to abolish the established form of empire and replace it with a new kind of monarchy, one modeled on the Hellenistic kingdoms where the ruler was divine. This would mean that a new "state cult" had been founded in what Willrich calls an act of "religious policy." In fact after his sojourn in Lyon Caligula did experiment with new forms of monarchy, which would have broken the paradoxical link between the emperor and the aristocratic hierarchy preserved from the time of the Republic. He borrowed elements from Hellenistic kingdoms, among which his identification with Alexander the Great was of particular significance, as can be seen from his horseback ride across the bay at Puteoli. Nevertheless there is important evidence against such an interpretation of his veneration as a god.

For one thing, he limited his appearances as a "god" to certain occasions. In a discussion of the emperor's clothing Dio writes that the special attire "was what he would assume whenever he pretended to be a god ... At other times he usually appeared in public in silk or in triumphal dress" (Dio 59.26.10). And Suetonius too mentions in addition to divine raiment the clothing of a *triumphator,* cloaks set with jewels or silken garments, in which the emperor allowed himself to be ordinarily seen. This fits with the specific reports on Caligula's behavior after the autumn of 40 (and before), since they make no mention at all of unusual dress, let alone symbols of divinity. Hence it was a case of individual appearances or public presentations rather than a permanent ceremonial practice, as one would expect if the aim had been to establish a "divinely ruled kingdom." Finally, evidence against the formal institution of a cult for a divine ruler is provided by the complete silence of the non-literary sources on the subject. Not a single inscription or coin mentions the emperor as a god in the context of the city of Rome or depicts him with emblems of divinity. In the evidence that survives, all honors awarded to Caligula or representations of him follow the patterns customary under his predecessors, Augustus and Tiberius.

Another explanation lies closer to hand. After his account of Vitellius's innovation in approaching the emperor, Dio relates the following incident: On a later occasion the emperor told Vitellius that he was in conversation with the moon goddess and asked whether he did not see the goddess near him. The singer Apelles had a similar experience when Caligula, who was standing next to a larger-than-life-sized statue of Jupiter, asked which of the two seemed greater to him, the emperor or the god. The meaning of the emperor's behavior can easily be interpreted if one recalls how he had dealt with insincere statements and flattery before, including the vows made when he fell ill in the year 37 and above all thereafter with regard to the "friendship" of the aristocracy since the year 39. Caligula exposed them all as lies by taking them at face value, and he humiliated the flatterer by cynically forcing him to do what he had announced. The pattern continues here. Neither Vitellius, who is notorious in the ancient sources for his servile flattery, nor Apelles actually believed Caligula was a god, and both of them knew that the emperor was aware of this. He reacted to being addressed as a god, which was intended as a gesture of submission, by compelling them to behave as if they really did take him for a god, that is, as if they were not in their right minds. Vitellius deftly managed to extricate himself from the awkward situation—an indication that he possessed the communicative skills required by the times. Trembling as if in awe, he dropped his gaze to the ground and replied softly, "Only you gods, Master, may behold one another" (Dio 59.27.6). Apelles, by contrast, who had fallen out of favor for unknown reasons after a period in Caligula's special grace, was at a loss for words. Caligula had him whipped, noting that even when the singer was screaming his voice retained its sweet sound.

As a group the senators seem to have fared much as Vitellius and Apelles did. Caligula did not reject the new form of their flattery as such, but cynically demanded that they then act as if he really were a god. We happen to know from a biographical account of Claudius that Caligula used membership in the priesthood of his cult to demand ruinous sums from leading senators. Thus the emperor's uncle "was forced to pay eight million sesterces to enter a new priesthood, which reduced him to such straitened circumstances that he was unable to meet the obligation incurred to the treasury; whereupon by edict of the prefects his property was advertised for sale to meet the deficiency, in accordance with the law regulating confiscations" (Suet. *Claud.* 9.2).

Some of the ancient sources themselves offer a different interpretation. They claim that the emperor, having lost his mind, took himself for a god and then forced the aristocracy to venerate his person accordingly. Modern biographers, too, have accepted this view, so that Caligula's "divinity" has played a decisive role in establishing his reputation as a mad emperor. How should this be judged?

First of all, it is telling that the earliest Roman sources, Seneca and Pliny the Elder, make no mention whatsoever that the emperor in his mental derangement considered himself a god, even though such assertions would have conformed perfectly with their no-holds-barred depiction of him as a misbegotten monster. The reason is evident: The claim would not have seemed very plausible to contemporaries. For one thing, they had lived through that time themselves, and doubtless wanted not to be reminded of their own disreputable role in his veneration as a god. Further, attributing divinity to the emperor as a way of flattering him had continued under Caligula's successors. Although Claudius forbade Romans to prostrate themselves before him or offer sacrifices to him, the author Scribonius Largus refers to him three times as "our god the emperor" (*deus noster Caesar*). After the Pisonian conspiracy under Nero in 65, the senator Cerialis, who had betrayed the conspirators, introduced a motion that a temple be built to the (living) emperor and a cult be established to venerate him.

Finally, both Seneca and Pliny reveal that they themselves were far from innocent of servility in their own dealings with emperors. Shortly after Caligula's death in 41 Seneca was banned by the new emperor Claudius for an adulterous affair with Caligula's sister Livilla; in his work dedicated to the emperor's freedman Polybius, which was written around this time, he attributes his escape from death to the "divine hand" of Claudius. In the forword to his *Natural History* (completed in 77) Pliny heaps extravagant praise on Vespasian's son Titus and says that Romans approach his father at morning receptions "with reverential awe"; he even goes so far as to compare his own work, which he dedicated to the prince, to offerings made to the gods. In the decades following Caligula's death, Roman aristocrats were far too caught up in the inflationary competition to praise the emperors themselves to consider or depict the cultic veneration of Caligula as a sign of madness—on the side of either the worshiped or the worshipers. But if this is so, how did the claim arise that Caligula believed in his own divinity?

Two other early authors—Philo and Josephus, who were Jewish—are the first to mention this subject. They left an account of Caligula because of a dramatic event in the history of the Jewish people in the last year of his rule. The emperor had given orders to dedicate the Temple in Jerusalem to his own cult and to place a larger-than-life-sized statue of himself there. It was a collision of two diametrically opposed views of religion. For Jews the desecration of their holiest site would have been the worst sacrilege imaginable, and it is Philo above all who pours out hatred for Caligula. From the Roman perspective, however, what was at stake was primarily a political matter. The cult of the emperor in the cities of the provinces was a demonstration of the local ruling class's political loyalty to Rome, which was welcomed in the capital, and rewarded.

Despite their partisanship the accounts of the two authors reveal that, as in other cases, the veneration of Caligula was not imposed from above but initiated from below. In 38 terrible pogroms against the Jewish population had occurred in Alexandria, and the non-Jewish residents of the city made a shrewd attempt to win support in high places by placing pictures of the emperor in synagogues and turning them into shrines for his cult. Avilius Flaccus, the prefect at the time, was too involved in Roman affairs to be able to act. His successor, Vitrasius Pollio, seems to have made no decision on the matter either, so both the Jewish and non-Jewish residents of Alexandria sent delegations to Caligula, the first of which was headed by Philo. The problem worsened and spread to Judaea, where similar unrest occurred (presumably around the middle of 40, although there is disagreement about the precise chronology). Jewish worshipers in the town of Jamnia destroyed an altar of the emperor's cult. From the Roman point of view this qualified as political rebellion, and it was only at this point that Caligula ordered Publius Petronius, the governor of Syria, to establish an imperial cult in the Temple in Jerusalem.

The whole episode had little to do with any ambitions of the emperor to be considered divine. This can be seen in the further course of the conflict. At first, Agrippa, the king of Judaea, who had been a member of Caligula's inner circle since the days in Lyon, was able to persuade him to rescind the order. When Petronius wrote that the Jews had threatened him with open insurrection, however, Caligula changed his mind again. The issue had now become one of enforcing Roman rule in the province, and he gave orders to proceed accordingly: to use all available military means to break Jewish resistance and to erect the statue of him in the Temple after all.

It is highly significant that both Philo, who discusses Caligula's mad belief in his own divinity at some length, and Josephus, who mentions it only briefly in three places, thereby become entangled in a fundamental contradiction. In Philo's detailed account of his two audiences with the emperor, Caligula is described as friendly, addressing the delegation formally about their business. At the second interview, after news of the Jewish uprising has arrived, he reproaches the delegation for the Jews' unwillingness to venerate him as a god—that was, of course, the fundamental problem—but his behavior is entirely normal then too. When shown into the emperor's presence, the Jewish delegates make deep, respectful bows, but Philo reports nothing about *proskynēsis*. Caligula next makes fun of the Jewish custom of eating no pork, and his entourage laughs in agreement. He is mainly concerned with giving instructions for furnishing of his living quarters in the gardens of Maecenas and Lamia on the Esquiline Hill, where the audience is taking place. He walks through the rooms, ordering expensive glass to be installed in the windows and paintings to be hung, with the Jewish and Greek delegations from Alexandria trailing around after him, up and down the stairs. He behaves, that is to say, like a perfectly normal Roman aristocrat occupied with the fittings and decor of his houses. His dilatory treatment of the two delegations is humiliating for them, of course, but in Philo's account Caligula shows not the slightest trace of a delusion that he is a god or, indeed, any other sign of insanity.

The same is true in the work of Josephus. In the historian's extensive narrative of the events leading up to Caligula's murder, the emperor is shown behaving completely normally. Josephus describes him offering a sacrifice to the deified Augustus, in whose honor games are being held on the Palatine Hill, and attending the theater with several trusted senators who occupy the seats around him and also accompany him when he leaves. Nothing in his dress or appearance differs in the least from that

of his aristocratic companions; there is no mention of any special ceremony and not a word of anything out of the ordinary in
the emperor's behavior. Philo and Josephus claim that Caligula
took himself for a god because he was insane, but their own
depictions of him do not support the claim. The reason for the
hostility in their accounts is not far to seek: It sprang from his
order to enforce the imperial cult in Jerusalem, which had plunged
Jews into extreme religious and political difficulties.

The first surviving Roman author who presents a similar
report is Suetonius, a hundred years after Caligula's death. In a
brief passage in his *Life of Gaius Caligula* he writes that the emperor
claimed "divine majesty" (*divina maiestas*) and instituted his own
worship. Suetonius also includes anecdotes intended to raise
doubts about the emperor's mental health: "At night whenever the
moon began to shine in full light he would regularly invite the
moon goddess into his bed and his embrace, while in the daytime
he would talk confidentially with Jupiter Capitolinus, now whis-
pering and then turning his ear to the mouth of the god, now in
louder and even angry language; for he was heard to make the
threat, 'Lift me up, or I will lift thee'" (Suet. *Cal.* 22.4).

By now the reader will not be surprised that Suetonius's
account is also on this occasion stamped with denunciatory intentions. In another text, however, the biographer himself provides
information that calls these remarks into question. In the passage
quoted above from his *Life of Vitellius,* Suetonius states explicitly
that it was the emperor Vitellius's father, Lucius, and not Caligula himself who initiated the veneration of him as a god. As it
happens, we have a parallel passage that reveals how Suetonius
adapted the information available to him and reworked the material. In his work *On Anger,* Seneca described a pantomime in
which Caligula took part, followed by a feast the emperor hosted

in the open air. When it was interrupted by thunder and light-
ning and the guests became alarmed, the emperor grew "angry
at heaven" and quoted a verse from Homer, "Lift me up, or I will
lift thee!" (*Iliad* 23.724). In other words he challenged Jupiter to a
wrestling match. Seneca considered this sacrilegious and called
Caligula demented for that reason. While the episode depicts
the emperor as an arrogant man with an explosive temper, it
does not in the least suggest that he was communicating with
Jupiter in a state of mental confusion. That is exactly how Suetonius reports it, however, taking the incident out of its original
context.

The story about the moon goddess can be similarly explained.
As shown above, the basis for it was a cynical joke intended to
demean the flatterer Vitellius. In Suetonius's account, though,
the emperor is depicted as suffering from a delusion that he is
actually in contact with the goddess. Suetonius has turned Caligula's own weapon against him: Just as the emperor pretended
to take his aristocratic flatterers seriously so as to expose how
mad their flattery was, now the biographer takes Caligula's jests
seriously, using them to portray him as insane. Nevertheless
there is a difference: The point of Caligula's joke could be grasped
by those present—its effect depended on that. In contrast, Suetonius's technique is not humorous at all. It extracts the emperor's
words from their original context so that their meaning is no
longer the same. The result is a misrepresentation of what really
occurred, but one that readers cannot immediately recognize as
such.

This is evident again a hundred years later in Cassius Dio.
On the one hand, he follows the opinion of Suetonius and takes
Caligula's divine adoration as evidence of his madness. On the
other hand he reports (from other sources that he, like Suetonius,

had available to him) a series of events in which the original context of the emperor's deification can still be recognized, and assembles information that contradicts the interpretation he adopted from Suetonius. Thus, for example, he reports the seriousness with which even the most prominent Romans venerated the emperor as a god, although it clearly amazes him. This procedure reduces the consistency of his account, but renders it all the more valuable as a source.

Returning now to the situation in Rome in the autumn of 40, we can see that the senators had not reckoned with Caligula's response to their conspiracies. They experienced a kind of humiliation they probably could not have imagined in their wildest dreams. The young man who was their ruler did not content himself with taking measures specifically designed to terrorize and dishonor them. He accepted the flatteries of individual senators and made the entire Senate venerate him as a god, treatment that alone would have represented extreme degradation for such an exalted group. But he did even worse: Counting on their submissiveness, he staged carnival-like performances at which they were forced to expose themselves to public ridicule by pretending they actually took the emperor in fancy dress for a god. Cassius Dio captured this bizarre way of shaming the highest-ranking members of Roman society in a vivid anecdote, although one suspects he may not have been entirely clear about what was going on. On one occasion when Caligula appeared on a stage costumed as Jupiter, there was a simple shoemaker from Gaul in the audience who burst out laughing. The emperor summoned him forward and asked: "What do I seem to you to be?" The shoemaker answered: "A big humbug." He suffered no consequences, since according to Dio the emperor would tolerate outspoken comments from the common people but not from men in important positions. But if one recalls the parallel situation with Vitellius, another interpretation of the scene suggests itself: Far from considering himself divine or intending to introduce an official emperor cult in Rome, Caligula was instead appearing as a god at occasional public performances to expose the senators' fearful and at the same time hypocritical submissiveness toward him in all its absurdity. And he did so before an audience of commoners who could not help laughing at the antics of the nobly born.

STABILITY OF RULE

The emperor's authority was uncontested. The soldiers of the Praetorian Guard—who were responsible for arrests, torture, and executions—profited from the prevailing conditions and were loyal to the emperor. Alongside them and sometimes in competition with them his Germanic bodyguards played an important role. As foreigners who did not speak Latin and hence were cut off from most contacts with other groups in Rome, they fixed their attention firmly on the emperor. By their constant presence they ensured his safety, and he paid them generously in return. Among the legions on the frontiers of the Empire, where little news arrived about conditions in Rome, the young emperor's popularity was unaffected. For them he remained the son of Germanicus, who had grown up in their camp and rewarded them so liberally at the start of his reign.

The people of Rome also continued to stand behind the emperor, who provided a generous supply of bread and circuses. Discord arose occasionally: When the people protested higher taxes Caligula sent out the Praetorian Guard, and he mocked the traditional relationship between the aristocracy and the commoners by sending old gladiators and injured men into the arena to fight against broken-down animals. This did not damage his popularity permanently, however, for he continued to sponsor "serious" games, and regularly distributed large sums of money. Josephus reports that the common people of Rome had an unfavorable opinion of the Senate and saw the emperor as their protection from the greed of the aristocracy.

The emperor's support among soldiers limited the threat that provincial governors from the senatorial order could pose to him. Moreover, Caligula's predecessors had already developed a new approach to the fundamental problem of rivalry with the aristocracy. There was an increasing tendency to choose "new men" from the equestrian order to fill positions that conferred extensive military power. Most of these appointees had excellent military and bureaucratic abilities, and they also owed their promotion, and consequent advancement into the highest rank of society, to the emperor. They enjoyed little prestige among aristocrats, commoners, or soldiers. All of this checked any danger of usurpation they might have represented. The recent failure of Lentulus Gaetulicus no doubt functioned as a curb on similar ambitions, and the recall of Lucius Vitellius from Syria proved that the emperor kept an eye on everything.

There were also senators in Rome who cooperated with the emperor and benefited from their ties to him. Various sources confirm that some of them maintained particular "friendships" with Caligula, attending his banquets, inviting him to their own, and accompanying him to public events such as theatrical performances. A few have already been mentioned. Vitellius had counted as a close friend of Caligula's since his diplomatic comment on the conversation with the moon goddess; he was the son of a man from the equestrian order who had served as a financial administrator under Augustus. His own son Aulus Vitellius, the later emperor, belonged to the emperor's inner circle as a *familiaris*. Quintus Pomponius Secundus, Caligula's co-consul at the start of 41 and the man who kissed the emperor's feet at a banquet, was the empress Caesonia's half brother. Gnaeus Sentius Saturninus was the son of a senator who had accompanied Germanicus, Caligula's father, on his journey to the East.

Gaius Sallustius Crispus Passienus, a well-known orator, is said to have enjoyed Caligula's special favor and to have accompanied him on his march to Germania. His father had been the first member of the family to achieve consular status, under Augustus. After that he had been adopted by the knight Gaius Sallustius Crispus, one of the closest confidants and most important political advisers of the first *princeps*. Later, under Claudius, he was married for a time to Agrippina, Caligula's sister and Claudius's niece (and later wife). Another member of Caligula's inner circle was Valerius Asiaticus. He came from the town of Vienna in the province of Gaul and owed his membership in the Roman Senate to the patronage of Antonia Minor, Caligula's grandmother, whom he had once courted at the same time as Lucius Vitellius. It appears that he was married to Lollia Saturnina, sister of the Lollia Paulina who was briefly Caligula's wife. Other documented members of the emperor's coterie in early 41 are Marcus Vinicius, Annius Vinicianus, and Paullus Arruntius. Vinicius had married Caligula's sister Julia Livilla in 33, but clearly had been able to thrive politically despite her banishment. His grandfather came from the equestrian order and rose to senatorial status as one of Augustus's most important generals. While Arruntius is otherwise unknown to us, Vinicianus was presumably Vinicius's nephew.

Some of these senators are reported to have been extraordinarily wealthy. None of them was descended from an old senatorial family of the Republican era; they had all risen to prominence in the Senate and the consulship through service to the emperor and as a result of his support. A few had been able to cement their position by marrying into his family. It was probably these men who took the lead in proposing flattering honors for Caligula and denouncing colleagues, and who procured themselves personal advantage through their proximity to the emperor and the opportunities for influence that resulted from it. In the case of Lucius Vitellius this is documented. Nonetheless their position was anything but pleasant. Claudius also was among Caligula's everyday associates, and just as he had to endure mockery and humiliation, so must the other members of this circle, as Vitellius and Pomponius did. The relationships between Caligula and these "friends" from the senatorial order were thus hardly characterized by mutual trust; here, too, communication ran in the customary ambiguous ways: In public they were submissive, but in fact, according to Josephus, they hated him. They were even aware of the others' hatred but did not dare to mention it, let alone initiate a conspiracy. While they maintained "friendly" relations with one another, they were full of suspicion and feared denunciation if they spoke out.

The center of power was occupied by others. Besides the empress Caesonia, the closest circle around Caligula comprised the two Praetorian prefects and freedmen like Callistus, Helicon, or Protogenes. What was true of the "new men" in the aristocracy was even truer for them: They owed their rise from obscurity to the emperor; he had been their path to enormous power and wealth, and they were accordingly hated by the aristocracy.

They were, so to speak, identified with the emperor, and there was little chance that they could survive his fall.

ALEXANDRIA AN ALTERNATIVE?

As we have seen, the emperor had a firm grip on power. All the same, toward the end of 40, many people in Rome were probably asking themselves how long things could go on this way. Caligula had been back in the city for four months, and he had used this time to attack the aristocrats of the senatorial order—forcing them to submit to him, exploiting them financially, humiliating them in personal relations, and exposing them to public ridicule. The odds that they could mount a successful conspiracy had dropped to near zero since the consulars' wives and children had been interned on the Palatine Hill. But what were the emperor's plans? At some point his revenge on the aristocracy for its attacks would have to be satisfied. What would come next?

Caligula must also have been asking himself questions about the future. He had already a year and a half earlier unmasked the ambiguity that had characterized communication between the emperor and the aristocracy since the time of Augustus in a way that made a return to it impossible. He had openly addressed the truth behind the aristocracy's public displays of obsequiousness— the fundamental rivalry between every emperor and high-ranking senators—most recently in jokes at the expense of Pompeius Magnus. He had likewise laid bare his own paradoxical position within the ranks of the aristocracy. He had long since ceased to envision Rome under imperial rule in the Augustan sense. Now he had chosen to destroy the old hierarchy and introduced a cult of his own worship. Was that a real alternative? Of course not, since he was using his deification largely as one more way to expose the senatorial aristocrats' self-abasement as hypocritical. It merely represented the high point of his campaign to dishonor them and confirmed at the same time that in reality no one venerated the emperor at all.

A second factor also came into play. The more time Caligula spent working to destroy the honor of aristocrats, the more he demonstrated how deeply his own position was embedded in Rome's aristocratic society. It must have been apparent that to make his superior position manifest and to enhance his own status he needed to degrade the others. In other words, he remained enmeshed in the old system of ranking precisely because he was so intent on abolishing it. His attempts to escape from the paradoxes of the emperor's role created new paradoxes, which perpetuated the old ones in inverted form. Was there a way out of such a quandary? Certainly not in Rome. There was no possibility of establishing a monarchy there, within political and social structures built up over centuries of Republican tradition.

In Philo's report on his legation to Caligula he mentions three times that the emperor was planning a journey to Alexandria, the city that the emperor had first seen as a child and where he had already been awarded great honors: "He was possessed by an extraordinary and passionate love for Alexandria. His heart was entirely set upon visiting it and on his arrival staying there for a very considerable time. For he thought this city was unique... and that its vast size and the worldwide value of its admirable situation had made it a pattern to other cities..." (Phil. *Leg.* 338). Philo ascribes part of Caligula's fascination with the city to the powerful influence of his servant Helicon, who was himself originally from Alexandria: "Elated with visions of that occasion when in the presence of his master and of almost the whole habitable world, since undoubtedly all the men of light and learning in the cities would journey from the furthermost parts to join in homage to Gaius, he [Helicon] would be honored by the greatest and most illustrious city of them all..." (Phil. *Leg.* 173). Philo also writes, however, that Caligula believed he could realize his wish to be venerated as a god there. The majority population of Alexandria had in fact enhanced its standing in his eyes by promoting the emperor's cult over the protests of the Jewish inhabitants. Josephus confirms that the emperor had plans to travel to Alexandria and reports that all the preparations had been completed by January of 41. Finally, Suetonius states that Caligula was then planning to move his residence and the imperial capital first to Antium, where he had been born, and afterwards to Alexandria.

Intentions of this kind were less aberrant than they might seem. Julius Caesar had stayed in Alexandria for a time, with Cleopatra. Before he was murdered, there were rumors that he wanted to leave Rome and concentrate the armed forces of the Empire in Alexandria (or Ilium), and that he would entrust the governing of Rome to his advisers. Marcus Antonius, Octavian's last great rival in the civil war and, like him, a great-grandfather of Caligula, had governed his part of the Empire from Alexandria and it is reported that he, too, had plans to make the city into a permanent capital. Last but not least, both Plutarch and Cassius Dio mention that as Nero's fall was approaching in the year 68 he intended to flee to Egypt and try to sustain his position from there.

In fact the city of Alexandria, the old capital of the Ptolemaic kings, was excellently suited as an alternative center of rule. According to Tacitus, one of Augustus's *dominationis arcana*, his "secret principles of domination," consisted of keeping Egypt for himself after the civil war. From then on senators and leading knights were prohibited from setting foot there without special permission. The old monarchical structures of the country remained intact, and the representative of the emperor governed through them in the role of a vice-king. Hence no one of senatorial rank was appointed as proconsul; prefects from the equestrian order were sent instead, as less likely to conceive thoughts of usurpation from the extent of their powers. In that era Egypt was the source of the Italian grain supply, so that—as Tacitus observes—it would have been easy to starve Italy from there. Furthermore, because of Egypt's geostrategic location it was possible to occupy and defend the country with a small force "against armies however formidable" (Tac. *Ann.* 2.59.3).

Egypt's special status was one part of Caligula's thinking. Another part derived from what he had experienced in his own short life. His first seven years as a member of his father's entourage in Germania and the East, his own campaigns in the North, his sojourns in Gaul and on the Gulf of Baiae—all these experiences had demonstrated that a Roman emperor could function as a mobile hub of government, so to speak, military and financial affairs included. With a minimum of military and administrative staff, he could collect taxes and draft recruits wherever he happened to be; he could carry out massive construction projects and display his power; he could correspond with cities and governors throughout the Empire, or receive delegations. Most importantly, Caligula had observed at close range that Tiberius served essentially unchallenged as Roman emperor even though permanently absent from Rome. For almost twelve years, from 26 until his death, he had resided on a small island and not set foot in the city. If it was possible to govern from Capri, why not from Alexandria, where the preconditions were considerably better?

Still it is possible that something quite different prompted Caligula to leave Rome. During the investigation of the most recent conspiracy, the senators' hatred for him had found expression in a scene he could not have anticipated. Caligula had intended to force Capito, father of the conspirator Betilienus Bassus, to witness the execution of his own son and finally threatened to kill him as well. Faced with death, Capito made a statement that took the weapons of denunciation and fear, which had prevailed in Caligula's hands up to that time, and turned them against the emperor: "Finding his life in danger, he pretended to have been one of the conspirators and promised to disclose the names of all the rest; and he named the companions of Gaius and those who abetted his licentiousness and cruelty." That is, he denounced Caligula's close aristocratic associates (probably the persons mentioned above), as well as his nonaristocratic aides, into which category people like Helicon or Protogenes must have fallen. "And he would have brought many to their deaths," as Cassius Dio reports, "had he not gone on to accuse the prefects, Callistus, and Caesonia, and so aroused disbelief." (Dio 59.26.7 [Zonaras]).

The people Capito denounced suffered no harm, and Capito was executed, but he had achieved his goal: Caligula began to harbor suspicions about his closest advisers and confidants, misgivings about the powerful people who both profited from his rule and served as its most important props. This is understandable, given his experiences a year earlier with his sisters and Aemilius Lepidus. Later, when he was alone—without his bodyguards—he sent for the prefects and Callistus and told them, " 'I am but one, and you are three; and I am defenseless, whereas you are armed. If, therefore, you hate me and desire to kill me, slay me!' When they fell at his feet and besought him, claiming that they had no such intention regarding him, he withdrew, pretending to be convinced. As a result of this affair, he believed that he was hated and that they were vexed at his behavior, and so he suspected them and wore a sword at his side when in the city; not only was he suspicious of their friendship, but they, also, on their side, were filled with fear. And to forestall any harmony of action on their part he attempted to embroil them with one another, by pretending to make a confidant of each one separately and talking to him about the others, until they understood his purpose..." (Dio 59.28.8).

Now the situation had become hazardous. The fates of Callistus and the Praetorian prefects were attached to the emperor. If he let one of them fall—or all of them, one after the other—there would be general rejoicing, at least within the Roman aristocracy. If the emperor himself were brought down, they would fall with him. With the power they wielded through their proximity to him, they could achieve all kinds of things, but there was one thing that remained beyond their reach. Callistus was a former slave, and the prefects had been knights of no particular distinction. Their social standing meant that they could not remove him and take his place. Their lack of social prestige had been precisely what qualified them for the offices they held. The most powerful men in the Empire after the emperor were now under pressure to act. If the emperor did not regain his confidence in them, they had only one option. Caligula too must have clearly recognized what that meant.

According to Josephus his departure for Alexandria was scheduled for 25 January 41. Who was to accompany him there and who to remain behind in Rome is not recorded.

FIVE

Murder on the Palatine

The great failed conspiracies of 39 opened and escalated the conflicts between Caligula and the Roman aristocracy. What they lacked, apparently, were conspirators—or at least no one wanted to admit having taken part in them. Instead, as we have seen, aristocratic historiography was at some pains to suppress all mention of them. For the conspiracy that led to the emperor's murder, the exact opposite is the case. The sources mention a strikingly large number of aristocrats' names, and there are even four different possible leaders to choose from. After identifying the core group, Cassius Dio goes on to say, "Nearly all the people around the emperor were won over, both on their own account and for the common good. And those who did not take part in the conspiracy did not reveal it when they knew of it, and were glad to see a plot formed against him" (Dio 59.29.1a).

One thing is certain: This is not how Caligula met his death. There was mutual distrust extending all the way into his innermost circle, as Dio reports himself, and a widespread willingness to denounce others—one may think of the scene of Protogenes

Figure 6. Coin depicting Caligula. RIC 37 (Gaius).

in the Senate not long before. In view of these circumstances, a conspiracy with many participants and many others in the know would not only have been extremely stupid; it would also undoubtedly have failed. The reason for the false information in the sources is obvious. After Caligula had been assassinated, men could gain credit as principled members of the aristocracy by claiming to have taken part in or known about the plot. At the same time they could wipe out the memory of the inglorious role they had actually played as hypocritical sycophants.

What actually occurred? Tacitus notes briefly that the emperor Gaius was murdered in "secret treachery" (*occultae insidiae*), in contrast to Julius Caesar, who was killed by a conspiracy of senators. All accounts are in agreement that the actual murder was committed by two tribunes of the Praetorian Guard, Cassius Chaerea and Cornelius Sabinus, with the assistance of a number of centurions, and that Callistus and the Praetorian prefects were informed about the plan in advance. Flavius Josephus, who provides the most detailed description, on the basis of a nearly contemporary senatorial history, identifies the architects of the conspiracy as one Aemilius Regulus of Cordoba (of whom nothing more is known) and Annius Vinicianus, along with Cassius Chaerea. In Josephus's own account of the murder itself, however, Regulus plays no role and Vinicianus plays a minor one. Many years later, people in Rome recalled Valerius Asiaticus as the most important leader of the conspirators, but this view is contradicted by Josephus and Dio's credible accounts of his actions after the murder. Furthermore, Josephus reports that more senators among the emperor's close associates knew about the planned assassination, but at the same time he writes that the murderers found pretexts to lure them away from the scene before killing the emperor; this obviously argues against the claim that they were aware of the plot.

Josephus provides one further piece of information, although he does not pursue its implications: Callistus, whom he depicts as Caligula's most powerful and universally feared adviser, not only participated in the conspiracy because he feared for his own life; he even attached himself to Claudius, "secretly going over to his side because he expected that in the event of Gaius's death the Empire would pass to him and that by laying up beforehand a store of favor and credit for his kindness he would have a basis for preferment and strength similar to what he now enjoyed" (Jos. *Ant.* 19.66). Callistus also claimed, according to Josephus, that he had been ordered by Caligula to poison Claudius but had found various excuses to delay. Josephus—almost certainly correctly—considers it unlikely that Callistus would have disobeyed such an order, but it does not occur to him that Callistus might nevertheless have claimed to Claudius that the order had been given.

A look at what happened after the murder rounds out the picture. Soldiers of the Praetorian Guard sought out Claudius, escorted him to their barracks, and proclaimed him emperor. Claudius immediately named Rufrius Pollio as new Praetorian prefect, removing from office the two men who had participated in the conspiracy. After the Senate recognized him as emperor the following day, one of his first acts was to get rid of Caligula's assassins. Chaerea was executed and Sabinus took his own life. Not long afterwards the two most important figures close to Caligula after Callistus, Protogenes and Helicon, were killed as well. And what about Callistus himself?

We know that Callistus *remained* a central figure under Claudius. In the *Annals* of Tacitus, which begin again in A.D. 47, as well as in the accounts of Suetonius and Cassius Dio, he is a powerful secretary *a libellis,* dealing with petitions to the emperor; he and two other freedmen—Narcissus and Pallas, who were responsible for correspondence and finances—"divided the power among themselves" (Dio 61[60].30.6b). Tacitus refers to Callistus's role in the assassination of Caligula, and characterizes him as someone who "had expert knowledge of the last court... and believed power to be held more securely by cautious than by vigorous counsels" (Tac. *Ann.* 11.29.2). The three men successfully deposed the empress Messalina in 48 and deliberated afterwards on who should succeed her; Callistus argued for Lollia Paulina, the former wife of Caligula. He was unable to prevent Agrippina, Caligula's sister, from becoming empress, but he did manage something very rare for people at the center of power in those days, emperors and empresses included: He died a natural death, about ten years after Caligula was murdered.

Back to January 41. No valiant senators eliminated the hated emperor. They had to leave the deed to Caligula's right-hand man, a former slave with power "no less than a tyrant's." The evidence suggests that events ran as follows: Callistus made use of his final option in order to save his own skin. An assassination of Caligula did not suffice by itself. It was necessary besides for a successor to be installed who was thereafter beholden. And the freedman could not have anything to do with the murder itself. No new emperor would have left his predecessor's killer unpunished, as that would set a dangerous precedent for his own security. The two Praetorian prefects must have accepted this option, although it was even more dangerous for them. Merely knowing of the assassination and doing nothing about it would mean a violation of the oath they had sworn to protect the emperor's life, and no successor could possibly have retained them in the positions they occupied. It can no longer be established what precise role they played, whether they failed to recognize the danger that a change of ruler represented for their own position, or whether it seemed a lesser threat than what they feared would happen if Caligula remained. They may have counted on a possible outcome that was in fact what actually happened: They were removed from office, but remained unharmed because they had helped to elevate the new emperor to the throne.

Choosing a successor was not a difficult task. The brother of Germanicus, Caligula's uncle, was the obvious candidate in dynastic terms and appeared harmless as well. The only task remaining was to find an assassin, someone either too dim to realize that he was letting himself in for certain death no matter how the attempt turned out, or else so motivated that he did not care.

The Praetorian tribune Cassius Chaerea is portrayed by Josephus as a kind of Roman hero of the old school, not only willing but eager to liberate Rome from the tyrant even if it cost him his life. Dio writes, however, that he was very old-fashioned and also had a personal motive for the murder. Supposedly Caligula had regularly made him the butt of jokes, teasing him as weak and unmanly; when he asked for the password of the day, Caligula would choose a word such as *Priapus* or *Venus.* Josephus provides further background information that depreciates the tribune's allegedly noble motives. He reports that Caligula had given Chaerea the distasteful task of collecting taxes, including demanding late payments, an assignment that no doubt made him unpopular. When he didn't perform it to the emperor's satisfaction, says Josephus, Caligula accused him of cowardice and insufficient manliness and began making jokes at his expense. "Even his fellow tribunes made fun of him; whenever he was to bring them the password from Caesar, they would mention beforehand one of the words that lend themselves to jests." Lastly the emperor "employed Chaerea in cases of murder and any others that called for torture, because he calculated that Chaerea's performance would be more cruel, since he would not want to be abused as a weakling" (Jos. *Ant.* 19.31, 19.34).

In other words, Chaerea was the man who did Caligula's dirty work. The emperor took advantage of his weaknesses and abused him for his own ends. Now Chaerea came under pressure from another direction. When Pomponius had been charged with crimes and the tribune had tortured Quintilia so brutally that even the emperor was overcome by pity, "these things grievously distressed Chaerea, for he had been, so far as it was in his power, a source of misery to persons who were considered even by Gaius to be deserving of consolation" (Jos. *Ant.* 19.37). Trying to demonstrate his masculinity when he was torturing a woman, he had proved himself to be more ruthless than the emperor; he could no longer excuse his actions by saying that he was merely carrying out Caligula's orders. It was this ill-omened situation that made Chaerea dare to bring up the subject of murdering the emperor, in a discussion with the Praetorian prefect Clemens and another tribune named Papinius. In addition to the unselfish motive of striking a blow for freedom Chaerea mentioned further arguments in favor of assassination, including the unsavory role they themselves played in the fate of Caligula' victims: "We pollute ourselves with shedding their blood and torturing them daily, up to the moment, mark you, when someone as Gaius's agent will do the same to us. For he will not favor us in his policy on account of these services, but will rather be governed by suspicion, especially when the number of the slain has increased . . . There we shall be, set up before him as targets, when we ought to be upholding the security and independence of all the people" (Jos. *Ant.* 19.42–43).

It is hardly likely that the Roman author whom Josephus is following here had a copy of Chaerea's speech at hand, and his reference to "daily" incidents of torture is a gross exaggeration. Nevertheless Josephus's assessment of the situation appears relatively accurate, precisely because it runs counter to his positive depiction of the conspirators. Fear had now gripped even the officers of the Praetorian Guard. The functionaries of power, the men responsible for torture and executions—led by Chaerea, the target of jokes about his lack of manliness—began to fear the emperor whose orders they carried out and to be concerned about their own fate. All the pieces of the plot had come together now, but obviously nothing had yet been decided.

Cassius Chaerea could hardly wait for it. Since he spent time in Caligula's presence, he saw many opportunities to kill him but people kept putting him off with flimsy excuses. The prefect Clemens told him that they would have to wait and hope for an opportune moment. Chaerea feared that the prefect might betray the plot and took Cornelius Sabinus into his confidence. He was willing to participate and strengthened Chaerea's resolve. All the same nothing happened, and the whole matter was delayed still further. Chaerea grew angry, reproached the others, and argued that they might miss the most favorable occasion. Although he had opportunities to strike every day, he did as he was told and held back. He was the sort of man who carried out orders, and that is what he did here. Finally the word came down that a favorable opportunity would be the theatrical performances in honor of Augustus scheduled for 21 to 24 January on the Palatine Hill. When the emperor entered the building that had been specially constructed for the plays, it would be easy to attack him.

What did that mean? Thousands of people would be assembled there, including the leading senators with their wives and children; naturally members of the Praetorian Guard and the emperor's Germanic bodyguards would be there, too. Attempting to assassinate the emperor in this setting entailed incalculable risks, as events would show. An attack at a banquet would have been far easier to manage, or even Chaerea's suggestion that Caligula be pitched off the palace roof when he was throwing money to the people. All this suggests that the prefects and Callistus, who was known for his caution, had not reached a final decision, or that the preparations for a smooth transition were not yet complete. But time was growing short. The emperor's departure for Alexandria was set for 25 January. Chaerea and Sabinus were kept waiting for three more days and finally given the go-ahead for 24 January.

The theater seems to have been located in the Area Palatina, a site on the hillside above the Forum. It had one exit into the city and one into the imperial palace. After the audience had been admitted and found their way through the crowd to their seats Caligula performed an animal sacrifice in honor of Augustus. Then he took his own seat, surrounded by the highest-ranking senators in his retinue, and gave orders for expensive sweets to be thrown to the spectators. On the program were a pantomime in which the leader of a band of robbers was nailed to a cross, and the tragedy of Cinyras and Myrrha. Both plays called for a good deal of imitation blood to flow on the stage. Shortly before one in the afternoon Caligula could not decide whether to stay till the end—since it was the last day of the performances—or to leave as usual for a bath and a meal and return later.

Chaerea, who was in readiness at the palace with the other officers participating in the conspiracy, could hardly endure the wait. He had already made up his mind that he would go into the theater and strike Caligula where he was sitting—meaning that he was prepared for the inevitable bloodbath among the senators and knights in the audience—when word suddenly came that Caligula and his entourage were entering the palace. Claudius, Marcus Vinicius, and Valerius Asiaticus were at the front of the group, followed by Caligula himself and Paullus Arruntius. On the pretext that the emperor wanted a moment of peace and quiet, the plotters kept the rest of his retinue from following. While Claudius and the two others proceeded along a main corridor lined with servants, Caligula, now flanked by Chaerea and Sabinus, turned into a side passage. It led to a room where Greek boys, sons of noble families, were rehearsing a performance to be given in his honor.

Different versions of the murder are reported. Suetonius offers two. As the emperor was speaking to the boys Chaerea, who was standing behind him, swung his sword with full force and hit him in the neck; then Sabinus stabbed him in the chest. The other version relates that Sabinus asked Caligula for the password and split his jaw as he turned around. As the emperor lay on the ground writhing in pain and shouting that he was still alive, all the other conspirators rushed forward and killed him with thirty further blows. In Josephus's account the "freedom fighter" Chaerea comes off somewhat better: Instead of attacking the emperor from behind he came at him in full view and struck a deep but not fatal wound. His sword pierced Caligula between the neck and shoulder and was stopped by his collarbone. Caligula neither shouted nor called for help, but only let out a loud groan and tried to flee. Then all the others fell on him with their swords. According to Seneca, Chaerea managed to decapitate the emperor with one blow, but many of the conspirators surrounded the emperor and thrust their swords into the corpse anyway.

Immediately following the murder Chaerea sent a tribune named Lupus to kill Caesonia and Drusilla, the emperor's young daughter. Reports say that the empress faced the blow courageously, and that the little girl was dashed against a wall. Then Chaerea and Sabinus, fearful of what would follow, fled into the interior of the palace complex and from there, by a different route, into the city.

Caligula was dead, but his power lasted for another few hours. The first to appear were his litter bearers, followed by members of his Germanic bodyguard. They seized several of the assassins and killed them on the spot, and also made short work of three senators who happened to be in the vicinity and fell into their hands. The bodyguards and Praetorian guardsmen went off in search of the other assassins, combing the corridors and rooms of the palace. In the theater spectators were horrified as news of what had happened spread. Rumors were rife: The emperor was wounded but not dead, and was receiving medical aid. Despite his wounds he had gone to the Forum, covered in blood, and was addressing the people. He wasn't dead at all, but had merely spread the rumor in order to test people's reactions. The senators who were hoping that the news was correct felt stunned and unable to move from their seats, but none of the others dared to stand up and leave the theater either, for fear that their action would be misinterpreted. Finally Germanic bodyguards who still hoped that the emperor was alive surrounded the theater with swords drawn. They placed the decapitated heads of the three dead senators on the sacrificial altar where everyone could see them. Now fear of death seized everyone. Some rushed toward the soldiers and fell on their knees, pleading that they had known nothing about an assassination attempt, if one had actually occurred. The soldiers should leave them in peace and go look for the people who were responsible for the outrage. "And so," writes Josephus, "even those who hated Gaius heartily and with justice were left with no chance to rejoice at his death, because they were on tenterhooks for fear of perishing with him..." (Jos. *Ant.* 19.144).

Imminent bloodbath was prevented by a well-known, wealthy auctioneer named Arruntius Euaristus. He entered the theater— at whose behest is not reported—in mourning attire and announced the death of Caligula in a loud voice. That put an end to the uproar among the *Germani*, since there was no emperor left for them to defend. With much pushing and shoving the theater emptied out.

Now Rome was without a ruler. At first the situation appeared to be in flux, but that impression was rapidly contradicted. Caligula belonged to the past, but the experiences and structures he left behind continued to determine behavior. The aroused populace streamed to the Forum, where popular assemblies took place, vigorously demanding that the murderers be punished. Despite the recent conflicts Caligula's popularity with the common people of Rome had remained intact. The senators attempted to take advantage of this favorable moment. The consuls called a session of the Senate in the Capitol and gave instructions for the contents of the emperor's treasury to be carried there immediately. The *cohortes urbanae*, who functioned as the city's police force, obeyed their orders and took up positions around the Capitol and Forum. In an agitated debate the senators fought over the future of Rome. Voices were raised calling for the end of imperial rule and the restoration of "freedom," meaning rule by the Senate in the style of the late Republic. Some senators even wanted to expunge the memory of all previous emperors and to destroy their temples. One of these was the consul Sentius Saturninus, who delivered a stirring speech. He portrayed Caligula as the culminating figure in a despotism that had been expanding since the days of Julius Caesar, declaring that imperial rule was tyranny and replaced freedom and law with the arbitrary will of an individual. He also recognized the senators' own role in all this, however: "This tyranny was fostered by nothing but indolence and our failure to speak in opposition to any of its wishes. We have succumbed to the seduction of peace and have learned to live like conquered prisoners. Whether we have suffered incurable disasters ourselves or have only observed the calamities of our neighbors, it is because we are afraid to die like brave men that we must endure being slain with the utmost degradation" (Jos. *Ant.* 19.180–81).

Saturninus had in fact been conspicuous for his servility to the emperor, since otherwise he would hardly have been serving as consul at the time. Josephus reports that after this speech another senator leaped to his feet and pulled from Saturninus's finger a ring with a likeness of Caligula on it, which identified him as a man in particularly high favor with the tyrant who had just been murdered. The rhetoric of freedom could little avail against the existing structures of power and modes of behavior that directed even the action of senators. In reality ambiguous communication within the aristocracy, which Caligula through his cynical behavior had allowed to run out, celebrated a joyous resurrection, and the debate was actually about who would become the new emperor. Three aspirants are mentioned by name. All three came from the group of senators who had maintained close contact with Caligula to the very end and who would also number among the favorites during Claudius's rule. Valerius Asiaticus's ambitions to succeed to the throne were thwarted by Annius Vinicianus, who had the same end in view for himself and tried to achieve it a year later: He was one of two central figures in the first great conspiracy against Claudius. The third aspirant was Marcus Vinicius, Caligula's brother-in-law. His move was blocked by the two consuls, Saturninus and Pomponius, who according to Dio had kissed Caligula's feet at a banquet only the day before. Presumably Saturninus's speech on freedom was aimed to position him as a possible candidate for emperor. The Senate debate encapsulates the paradox of the era, which had dominated Caligula's brief reign and that he had set himself against in a new fashion: No one wanted an emperorship, but everyone wanted to be emperor.

If even senators could come to no agreement about "freedom," then others were even less able to do so. As the Senate session dragged on and on, new facts had long since been created on the ground. The regular soldiers of the Praetorian Guard, who had known nothing about the conspiracy, had rushed here and there excitedly for a while hunting the emperor's killers, and then gathered to discuss further steps. This was probably the moment the two prefects had been waiting for, when they would take center stage. Understandably the Guard had no interest in rule by the Senate, nor did they want to wait for the Senate to choose a claimant to the throne. Their own importance would increase if they created the emperor themselves. They quickly agreed on Claudius, who benefited from the soldiers' loyalty to the dynasty. The guards discovered him hiding on the Palatine Hill, where he had sought safety in the uproar; they proclaimed him emperor in the Area Palatina and then took him to the Praetorians' camp. The idea of Republican "freedom" was rejected in the Forum as well, for the people also backed Claudius, hoping in that way to avoid a battle over the succession and the threat of civil war.

Envoys were sent back and forth between the Senate and the Praetorians' camp, and it is said that King Agrippa of Judaea, Caligula's close associate, skillfully advocated Claudius's cause. In the middle of the night the balance of power tipped definitively in his favor. Only one hundred senators were present in the Senate; the others had cautiously retreated to their homes. In the end the urban cohorts joined the Praetorian Guards and backed Claudius, too. The few hours in which the senators had believed they had power were over, and now their fear of the new emperor was beginning to grow.

The next morning Claudius was escorted into the palace. He announced a donative of 15,000 (or 20,000) sesterces for every Praetorian. The Senate recognized him as emperor and awarded him the customary rights and honors. Cassius Chaerea, Lupus, and the centurions who had participated in the assassination were executed, and Sabinus committed suicide. Reportedly it was Agrippa who disposed of Caligula's badly mutilated corpse, taking it to the Lamian Gardens and interring it in a makeshift grave.

Inventing the Mad Emperor

"The histories of Tiberius and Caligula, of Claudius and Nero,"
writes Tacitus at the start of his *Annals*, "were falsified through
cowardice while they flourished, and composed, when they fell,
under the influence of still rankling hatreds" (Tac. *Ann.* 1.1.2). The
denunciatory devaluation that followed the emperors' deaths
formed a perfect counterpart to the servile adulation they enjoyed
during their lifetimes. But this alone does not mean that the
Roman aristocracy was made up of morally inferior people. Or
to put it more precisely: Moral categories are unsuitable here—
just as in the case of the emperors also—to explain what occurred.
The senators were victims of a clash between new circumstances
and their old ways of behaving, which no longer fit. The few who
were unwilling to come to terms with imperial rule—or who
wished to be emperor themselves—tried their hand at conspiracy
and only made matters more complicated. Those who were most
successful at adapting the traditional aristocratic striving for
power and honor to the new circumstances acquired a bad reputation as opportunists. Occasionally the same people managed to

stand out in both groups. Once someone had set flattery on the path of runaway inflation, the others had no choice but to join in and go along.

Under Caligula the senators had been confronted with unprecedented experiences. They could not accuse him of committing murder arbitrarily; instead he had simply let them give free rein to their servility and cynically taken it at face value. He had held up a mirror to the Roman aristocracy and showed them the absurdity of their own behavior. In so doing he had made them look ridiculous and let them humiliate themselves as never before. Utterly powerless, they had been forced to tolerate his game and join in it. What form did their "still rankling hatred" take after his death?

A good clue is available in the speech given in the Senate by consul Sentius Saturninus after the assassination, which Josephus quotes from his Roman source. The consul fell back on a long-standing pattern and accused Caligula of extreme tyranny. Clearly it never crossed anyone's mind to call him insane. Why should it have? The men leading the debate in the Senate had remained the emperor's aristocratic followers until the end, and if they had advanced the implausible claim that they had been serving a madman, they would have only created new embarrassments for themselves and the aristocracy as a whole.

Seneca is the first to speak of Caligula's madness (*furor* and *insania*) in his writings, which date from not long afterwards. If one examines these passages more closely, however, it emerges that he is not passing judgment on the deceased emperor's mental health, but is rather filled with hatred and accusing him of tyrannical behavior and the annihilation of freedom. He deplores the ignominy that this has brought on the Roman Empire. Seneca uses "insanity" as a term of abuse, to censure immorality and the violation of all aristocratic conventions. He uses the term in a similar sense when he speaks of women so extravagant that they wore earrings worth more than the combined fortunes of two or three aristocratic families. Finally, it is noteworthy that in various places in his writings he excoriates Alexander the Great in almost exactly the same language, as an "insane" and "megalomaniacal" young man—a parallel to which Caligula would have had no objection.

In the writings of the Jewish authors Philo and Josephus, the allegation of *mania* is directly connected to Caligula's demand that he be venerated as divine. Here, too, the word is used in a derogatory sense to reflect what Jews regarded as blasphemy on the emperor's part and the threats to the Jewish people that had arisen from this. As we have seen, the emperor himself shows no signs of psychopathology in the descriptions of either author; on the contrary, Philo recognizes his particular psychological skill in seeing through the motives of his interlocutors, while Josephus credits him with superior rhetorical abilities.

Pliny the Elder, who refers to Caligula's *insania*, uses the word in the context of the emperor's construction projects in Rome and goes on to note in the same sentence that his "insanity" was surpassed by Marcus Scaurus, Sulla's stepson, whose houses were even more luxurious and extravagant. Tacitus refers to the "troubled brain" (*turbata mens*) of the emperor but goes on to say that "it did not affect his power of speech" (Tac. *Ann.* 13.3.2). Tacitus is also intent on pronouncing a moral verdict against the emperor, as appears in the other passages where he mentions Caligula. He repeatedly uses such terms as "capriciousness," "malice," "dissimulation," "cunning," and "irascibility." It is thus not surprising that Caligula is by no means the only emperor who was called "insane." The same description was applied to Tiberius, Claudius, and Nero.

Who came up with the idea that Caligula was truly mentally ill? Among the extant works by ancient authors it is Suetonius who raises the claim first. The emperor, he writes, was in poor health both physically and mentally. He suffered from epilepsy as a child and later from sudden attacks of fainting as well. Sudden fits of anxiety, severe insomnia, and confused images in dreams plagued him. Suetonius reports further that Caligula was aware of his own mental illness and reflected on possibilities for "clearing his brain" (*de purgando cerebro*). Thus it was almost a century before the term of abuse was reified and the Roman aristocracy that had suffered under Caligula received this dubious restitution of its honor. And the diagnostician was not a senator but a former imperial secretary from the equestrian order, who pursued antiquarian studies and studded his biographies of the emperors with anecdotes. He explains Caligula's condition by adding the comment: "It is thought that his wife Caesonia gave him a drug intended for a love potion, which however had the effect of driving him mad" (Suet. *Cal.* 50.2).

It remains an open question how much Suetonius added to the invention of the mad emperor and how much he borrowed from earlier documents (containing expressions of fresh hatred that historians like Tacitus did not consider worth passing on). What we do know is that his biography of Caligula decisively influenced the way the emperor was perceived from then on. Suetonius composed it at a time when, after more than a century of bloody conflicts between emperors and aristocracy, peace and a spirit of accommodation defined their relations. Rulers from Nerva to Marcus Aurelius (A.D. 96–180) displayed aristocratic modesty, and the senatorial aristocracy seems to have learned to live with imperial rule, which had taken on a form they could

endure. In these circumstances the memory of an emperor who
had tried to establish an undisguised monarchy, who had humiliated aristocrats and given them a taste of what imperial power
really meant, must have been very annoying. It was much more
pleasant to declare that if an emperor strove to create a monarchy
he was a mentally diseased tyrant, who rightly and necessarily
came to a dreadful end. Suetonius's contemporaries in the second
century saw precisely this intention in his biography of Caligula;
this is demonstrated by the fate of a Roman in the time of the
emperor Commodus, which bears a certain resemblance to the
experience of Ludwig Quidde nearly two thousand years later.
When the son of Marcus Aurelius came to the throne at the age
of nineteen and was confronted right at the start of his reign with
a conspiracy among the leaders of the senatorial aristocracy, the
existing accommodation came to an abrupt end. Force and undisguised autarchy once again shaped the age. Commodus, it is
reported, had someone thrown to wild beasts to be devoured
because the man had read Suetonius's *Life of Gaius Caligula*.

Commodus was murdered, too, and the message of Suetonius's biography of Caligula lent his portrait plausibility in the following centuries. In an abbreviated late-fourth-century history of
the emperors the section on Caligula describes his cruelty, incest,
and declaration of his own divinity, and then continues: "Perhaps
it would have been more fitting not to preserve this for posterity.
It is useful to know all the actions of the emperors, however, so
that the bad ones among them may avoid similar deeds, if only
out of fear for their reputation in future generations" (*Epitome de
Caesaribus* 3.6). The writer of this passage was unaware that the
kind of monarchy envisioned by Caligula had more than a little
similarity to the imperial rule of his own day: From the reigns of

Diocletian (284–305) and Constantine (324–37), emperors appeared in jewel-studded robes and were venerated in a complicated ceremony requiring aristocrats to prostrate themselves and kiss the hem of the imperial purple robe. And the emperors had also deserted Rome, leaving behind the senatorial society there and establishing a new center of rule in Constantinople.

That was a long way in the future, however, along a path that led from the peace of the second century to the turmoil of the third. But how did matters proceed in Rome in the year 41? How did Claudius conduct himself, who—similarly as had Caligula—suddenly became Roman emperor after years spent in subjection and danger? His first actions corresponded quite closely to those of his hated nephew four years earlier, and he dealt with his deceased predecessor in very much the same way that Caligula had dealt with Tiberius. Once again the aim was to make a break with the past. While he was still in the Praetorian Guard's barracks Claudius promised the senators that he would share power with them. He declared that trials for *maiestas* would not be permitted in the future and summoned the people whom Caligula had banned back to Rome. Most of the measures Caligula had introduced in the previous year were rescinded; *proskynēsis* before the emperor and sacrifices to him were prohibited. Members of the old noble families were allowed to wear their special honorific insignia, but once again the successor was able to prevent a *damnatio memoriae,* the elimination of all reminders of his predecessor from the public sphere. Only Caligula's portraits were removed from the city, and later the Senate was allowed to decide to melt down coins on which the murdered emperor was depicted. Amnesty was declared for everything that had been said or done in the hours between the end of the old reign and the establishment of the new one. The aristocratic circle around the emperor continued to consist largely of the same men as under Caligula: In the following years Marcus Vinicius, Valerius Asiaticus, and Passienus Crispus received the honor of a second consulate, while Lucius Vitellius achieved even a third one.

The reader will not be surprised that all that on this occasion also availed nothing. Within less than a year the first conspiracy against Claudius was mounted, and it resembled the great conspiracy of mid-39. This time the central figures were Annius Vinicianus in Rome and the governor of Dalmatia, Arruntius Camillus Scribonianus. Once more members of the senatorial aristocracy participated in large numbers. The uprising failed because the troops refused to take up arms in a civil war. The new emperor, who was fifty at the time of his ascent to the throne, had learned a thing or two, however. Every visitor had to undergo a body search before being admitted into his presence. When the emperor paid ailing, bed-ridden senators the honor of a visit, the rooms of the house were thoroughly inspected first, and every blanket and pillow was carefully examined. The importance of freedmen as trusted figures in the emperor's entourage continued to grow. A second attempt was made to conquer Britain, this time with success. But none of that helped either. Unlike in Caligula's time, a number of years later a conspiracy within the family succeeded, with Agrippina again at the center of it. Claudius, having recalled her from banishment and later brought her to the palace as his wife, died after Agrippina served him a dish of poisoned mushrooms so that her son Nero could become emperor.

And what was the reaction of the aristocracy to Claudius's demise? Seneca, who had been accustomed to expressing his gratitude for the emperor's "divine hand," wrote a biting satire on him almost before the body was cold, and expressed what everyone was thinking. If Caligula, who had dared aspire to founding a monarchy in plain view in Rome, was condemned posthumously as a "madman," then Claudius, who had tried to spare the aristocracy, was known after his death as a "fool."

Epilogue to the English Edition

"Mad emperors are an embarrassment to serious historians," as the ancient historian Catherine Edwards once aptly observed (*Classical Review* 41 [1991]: 407). On the other hand they hold a special fascination for a broader public with an interest in history, as can clearly be seen from the success of popular biographies, historical novels, or spectacular films. The present biography of Caligula takes this as its point of departure and has two aims. The brief life of this emperor is narrated in a form that preserves the tension and drama of events as they unfolded and that is meant to be accessible to general readers. At the same time an attempt has been made to solve the historical problem this emperor presents with a new interpretation.

The narrative approach chosen has required the exclusion of two elements: Competing hypotheses of modern scholars, to which this book owes a great deal, are discussed only in a few exceptions, and there is no systematic presentation of my own theory of politics, society, and patron-client relationships in the early Roman Empire, on which the interpretation is based. Instead the endnotes list citations from ancient sources important for my own line of argument, and central scholarly works are collected in the bibliography. Both are intended to enable the public (both with and without previous knowledge of the field) to look up references and pursue further reading.

I had the first opportunities to discuss my hypotheses on Caligula with students in two seminars at the universities of Munich and Bielefeld, and then in the context of talks delivered at the Kulturwissenschaftliches Institut in Essen and at the universities of Basel, Bielefeld, Freiburg im Breisgau, Greifswald, and Münster. I have profited from comments and suggestions. Tanja Schaufuß, Katharina Stüdemann, Fabian Goldbeck, Bert Hildebrand, Jan Meister, and Dirk Schnurbusch were of great help to me in preparing the manuscript.

The very positive reactions to the book from both critics and the public, and the translations into Italian, Spanish, and Dutch have confirmed my belief that serious historical scholarship with a theoretical foundation certainly goes well together with a dramatic narration of events. I am very pleased that the University of California Press is now publishing an English edition that has been revised and slightly expanded.

Aloys Winterling
Berlin, March 2011

NOTES

INTRODUCTION: A MAD EMPEROR?

Caligula as a monster: Suetonius, *Gaius Caligula*, 22.1; **extravagance:** ibid., 37; **sex life:** ibid., 24.36, 41.1; **cruelty:** ibid., 27; **the consuls:** ibid., 26.3; **veneration as a god:** ibid., 22.2–4; **his horse:** ibid., 55.3; **Alexandria:** ibid., 49.2. **Caligula's insanity:** Seneca, *On Anger (De Ira)*, 1.20.9, 3.19.3, 3.21.5; Philo, *The Embassy to Gaius*, 76, 93; Pliny, *Natural History*, 36.113; Josephus, *Jewish Antiquities*, 18.277, 19.1, 19.193; Tacitus, *Annals*, 13.3.2; Suetonius, *Gaius Caligula*, 50.2, 51.1; Dio, *Roman History*, 59.26.5; **modern scholarship:** Quidde, "Caligula," 67; Ferrill, *Caligula*, 165; Yavetz, "Caligula," 105. **Tacitus on Agrippina:** *Annals*, 14.2; cf. Josephus, *Jewish Antiquities*, 19.204. **Suetonius on the conspiracy of** A.D. **39:** *Claudius*, 9, and *Vespasian*, 2.3; Celsus, *De Medicina*, 3.18–22; Siegel, *Galen on Psychology*, 163; Flashar, *Melancholie*, 130–31. **Insanity in the law: on homicide:** Justinian, *Digest*, 1.18.13.1, 1.18.14, 29.5.3.11, 48.8.12. **Violations of the *lex maiestatis:*** Justinian, *Digest*, 48.4.7.3; *Codex Justinianus*, 9.7.1. **Libel:** Justinian, *Digest*, 9.2.5.2, 47.10.3.1. **Mad rulers of later times:** Middlefort, *Mad Princes*.

CHAPTER I. CHILDHOOD AND YOUTH

The Legacy of Augustus

Dates of Caligula's life and reign: Kienast, *Kaisertabelle*, 85–86.
Contemporaries' opinion of Augustus: Tacitus, *Annals*, 1.9–10.
Introduction of the monarchy through the restoration of the Republic: Meier, "C. Caesar Divi filius."

The Political Family

Mommsen, *Staatsrecht* 2.1143. **The Julio-Claudian dynasty:** Cf. Kienast, *Kaisertabelle*, 61–100; Meise, *Julisch-claudische Dynastie*.

A Childhood as "Little Boots"

Popularity of Germanicus: Suetonius, *Gaius Caligula*, 3–6. **The nickname and situation in the legionaries' camp:** Seneca, *On the Firmness of the Wise Man* (*De Constantia Sapientis*), 18.4; Tacitus, *Annals*, 1.41–44, 1.69.4; Suetonius, *Gaius Caligula*, 9; Dio, *Roman History*, 57.5.6–7; cf. the *Life of Commodus* (10.2) in the *Historia Augusta*. **The journeys to Greece and the East:** Tacitus, *Annals*, 2.53–61, 2.69–72; Suetonius, *Gaius Caligula*, 10.1, and *Tiberius*, 52.2–3. **The city of Assos:** Smallwood, *Documents*, no. 33, p. 29, ll. 15–17. **Germanicus's funeral procession:** Tacitus, *Annals*, 2.75.1, 3.1–5.

Conditions in Ancient Rome under Tiberius

Cf. Levick, *Tiberius*. **Salutatio at the houses of Augustus and Tiberius:** Winterling, *Aula Caesaris*, 122–23. **Trials for maiestas:** Tacitus, *Annals*, 3.37.1, 3.38.1–2, 3.65–70; Suetonius, *Tiberius*, 58; Dio, *Roman History*, 57.23. **On Titius Sabinus:** Tacitus, *Annals*, 4.184, 4.68–70; Dio, *Roman History*, 58.1.1b. **Capri:** Tacitus, *Annals*, 4.67; Suetonius, *Tiberius*, 40; Dio, *Roman History*, 58.1.1. **Sejanus's salu-**

tatio: Dio, *Roman History,* 57.21.4, 58.5.2. **Consulship through Sejanus:** Tacitus, *Annals,* 4.68.2. **Sejanus's power, honors, and downfall:** Tacitus, *Annals,* 4.74; Suetonius, *Tiberius,* 65; Dio, *Roman History,* 58.4–11. **Tiberius's fearfulness:** Suetonius, *Tiberius,* 63, 65–66.

A Perilous Youth

The poisoning of Drusus (II): Tacitus, *Annals,* 4.7, 4.8.1. **Nero and Drusus (III):** Tacitus, *Annals,* 4.8.3–4, 4.17.1–2; Suetonius, *Tiberius,* 54. **Enmity toward Agrippina and her sons:** Tacitus, *Annals,* 4.12, 4.17.3; Suetonius, *Tiberius,* 54. **Intrigue against Agrippina at Tiberius's dinner:** Tacitus, *Annals,* 4.54; Suetonius, *Tiberius,* 53.1. **Intrigues against Nero:** Tacitus, *Annals,* 4.60. **Arrest of Agrippina and Nero:** Tacitus, *Annals,* 4.67.3–4. **Caligula in the house of Livia and Antonia:** Suetonius, *Gaius Caligula,* 10.1. **Caligula's funeral oration for Livia:** Tacitus, *Annals,* 5.1.4. **Death of Nero:** Suetonius, *Tiberius,* 54.2, 61.1; Dio, *Roman History,* 58.8.4. **Treatment of Drusus (III):** Tacitus, *Annals,* 6.23.2, 6.24, 6.40.3; Dio, *Roman History,* 58.3.8. **Intrigues and charges against Caligula:** Tacitus, *Annals,* 6.3.4, 6.5.1, 6.9.2.

Capri and the Path to the Throne

Caligula moves to Capri: Suetonius, *Gaius Caligula,* 10.1. **Supposed chances for the throne:** Dio, *Roman History,* 58.8.1–2. **Dynastic prestige of Germanicus's family:** Tacitus, *Annals,* 5.4.2; Suetonius, *Tiberius,* 65.2. **Avillius Flaccus:** Philo, *Against Flaccus,* 9–11. **Death of Drusus:** Tacitus, *Annals,* 6.23–24; Suetonius, *Tiberius,* 54. **Death of Agrippina:** Tacitus, *Annals,* 6.25; Suetonius, *Tiberius,* 53.1. **Julius Agrippa and Caligula:** Josephus, *Jewish Antiquities,* 18.161–69, 183–92. **The grammarian Seleucus:** Suetonius,

Tiberius, 56. **Caligula's education:** Josephus, *Jewish Antiquities,* 18.206. **Tiberius's scholarly interests:** Suetonius, *Tiberius,* 70–71. **Caligula's quaestorship:** Dio, *Roman History,* 58.23.1. **Wedding in Antium:** Tacitus, *Annals,* 6.20; cf. Dio, *Roman History* (58.25.1), who places the event in the year 35. **M. Junius Silanus:** Tacitus, *Annals,* 3.57.1; Dio, *Roman History,* 59.8.5–6. **Marriages of Caligula's sisters:** Tacitus, *Annals,* 6.15; Dio, *Roman History,* 58.20.1. **Tiberius's will:** Suetonius, *Tiberius,* 76. **Macro's support, the affair with Ennia:** Philo, *The Embassy to Gaius,* 32–33, 39–40, cf. 61; Suetonius, *Gaius Caligula,* 12.2; Tacitus, *Annals,* 6.45.3; Dio, *Roman History,* 58.28.4. **Tiberius's last plans for the succession and risk for Caligula:** Philo, *Against Flaccus,* 11–12, and *The Embassy to Gaius,* 24–25, 41, 58; Suetonius, *Tiberius,* 62.3; Dio, *Roman History,* 57.22.4b, 58.23.2; Josephus, *Jewish Antiquities,* 18.211–15; Tacitus, *Annals,* 6.46.3. **Death of Tiberius:** Tacitus, *Annals,* 6.50; Suetonius, *Tiberius,* 72–73, and *Gaius Caligula,* 12.2; Dio, *Roman History,* 58.28.3.

CHAPTER 2. TWO YEARS AS PRINCEPS

A Young Augustus

The journey to Rome: Suetonius, *Gaius Caligula,* 13–14. **Caligula's first speech in the Senate:** Dio, *Roman History,* 59.6.1–3. **The first denunciation for conspiracy:** Suetonius, *Gaius Caligula,* 15.4. **Tiberius's funeral:** Dio, *Roman History,* 59.3.7–8; Suetonius, *Gaius Caligula,* 15.1. **Tiberius's bequests:** Dio, *Roman History,* 59.2; Suetonius, *Gaius Caligula,* 16.3. **On the drills of the Praetorian Guard:** Dio, *Roman History,* 59.2.1. **Burial of Caligula's mother and brothers:** Suetonius, *Gaius Caligula,* 15.1; Dio, *Roman History,* 59.3.5. **Honors for his family:** Suetonius, *Gaius Caligula,* 15.2–3; Dio, *Roman History,* 59.3.3–4. **Adoption of Gemellus:** Philo, *The Embassy to Gaius,* 26–27; Dio, *Roman History,* 59.1.3. **Renunciation**

of honors: Dio, *Roman History*, 59.3.1, 59.4.4, 59.6.5. **Greeting ritual:** Dio, *Roman History*, 59.7.6.

Illness and Consolidation

Drusilla and Lepidus: Suetonius, *Gaius Caligula*, 24.1; Dio, *Roman History*, 59.22.6–7. **Caligula's illness:** Philo, *The Embassy to Gaius*, 14; Suetonius, *Gaius Caligula*, 14.2; Dio, *Roman History*, 59.8.1. **The murder of Gemellus:** Philo, *The Embassy to Gaius*, 23, 29–31; Suetonius, *Gaius Caligula*, 23.3; Dio, *Roman History*, 59.8.1 and 3. **The fall of Macro:** Philo, *The Embassy to Gaius*, 58–61; Suetonius, *Gaius Caligula*, 26.1; Dio, *Roman History*, 59.10.6–7 (Dio's chronology is confused). **M. Arrecinus Clemens:** *Prosopographia Imperii Romani*², A 1073. **Execution of further supporters of Gemellus:** Dio, *Roman History*, 59.8.1, 59.10.7–9. **Avillius Flaccus:** Philo, *Against Flaccus*, 9–10. **Silanus:** Suetonius, *Gaius Caligula*, 23.3; Dio, *Roman History*, 59.8.4–6. **Reasons for aristocrats' suicides:** Tacitus, *Annals*, 6.29. The chronological order for the downfall of Macro and Silanus follows Philo's account. **Marriage:** Suetonius, *Gaius Caligula*, 25.1; Dio, *Roman History*, 59.8.7–8 (where the bride's name is given as Cornelia Orestina). **New Year's oaths,** *rationes imperii*, **works on history, the courts, the equestrian order:** Suetonius, *Gaius Caligula*, 16.1–2; Dio, *Roman History*, 59.9.1–2 and 4–5. **Reintroduction of popular elections:** Suetonius, *Gaius Caligula*, 16.2; Dio, *Roman History*, 59.9.6, 59.20.3–6. *Collegia:* Dio, *Roman History*, 60.6.6. **Games in the year 38:** Dio, *Roman History*, 59.10.1–5; Suetonius, *Gaius Caligula*, 18.1; cf. 21. **Honors for Caligula:** Suetonius, *Gaius Caligula*, 16.4. **Agrippa's close friendship with Caligula:** Philo, *The Embassy to Gaius*, 268. **Deaths of flatterers:** Dio, *Roman History*, 59.8.3–4; Suetonius, *Gaius Caligula*, 27.2.

Holding Power

Aristocratic households: Rilinger, "Domus und res publica."
Ceremony at the *salutatio:* Seneca, *On Favors* (*De Beneficiis*),
6.33–34. **Bequests in Tiberius's will:** Suetonius, *Gaius Caligula,*
37.3; Dio, *Roman History,* 59.2.6. **Caligula's buildings on the Pal-**
atine: Winterling, *Aula Caesaris,* 57–59. **Presence of Agrippina**
and others at the *salutatio:* Philo, *The Embassy to Gaius,* 261–62,
267. **Macro's admonition at banquet:** Philo, *The Embassy to*
Gaius, 42–44. **Order of seating at table:** Suetonius, *Gaius Calig-*
ula, 24.1, and *Claudius,* 8. **Guests at Caligula's banquets:** Suetonius, *Gaius Caligula,* 55.2, 32.3, 36.1–2, and *Vespasian,* 2.3. **Foods**
served: Suetonius, *Gaius Caligula,* 37.1. **Expenditure by aristo-**
crats: Pliny, *Natural History,* 9.117. **Cleopatra:** Pliny, *Natural His-*
tory, 9.119–20. **Macro's admonitions about behavior in public:**
Philo, *The Embassy to Gaius,* 45–46. **Gaianum:** Dio, *Roman History,*
59.14.6. **Vitellius:** Suetonius, *Vitellius,* 4, 17.2. **Caligula as a glad-**
iator: Suetonius, *Gaius Caligula,* 32.2, 54.1; Dio, *Roman History,*
59.5.5. **Apelles and Mnester:** Dio, *Roman History,* 59.5.2; Suetonius, *Gaius Caligula,* 36.1, 55.1. **Augustus at games:** Suetonius,
Augustus, 43.2–3. **Caligula's behavior at games:** Dio, *Roman His-*
tory, 59.5.4, 59.13.5.

The Death of Drusilla

Caligula in mourning: Seneca, *On Consolation* (*Ad Polybium de*
Consolatione), 17.4–5; Suetonius, *Gaius Caligula,* 24.2. **Posthumous**
honors for Drusilla: Dio, *Roman History,* 59.11; Suetonius, *Gaius*
Caligula, 24.2. **Drusilla's ascension to heaven:** Seneca, *Apocolo-*
cyntosis, 1.2; Dio, *Roman History,* 59.11.4. **Caligula's marriage to**
Lollia Paulina: Suetonius, *Gaius Caligula,* 25.2; Dio, *Roman His-*
tory, 59.12.1, 59.23.7; Tacitus, *Annals,* 12.2.2.

The Empire

Caligula's journey to Sicily: Josephus, *Jewish Antiquities,* 19.205–6; Suetonius, *Gaius Caligula,* 20, 21.1, 51.1. **Fire in Rome:** Dio, *Roman History,* 59.9.4. **Aqueducts:** Frontinus, *On Aqueducts (De Aquaeductibus Urbis Romae),* 13; Suetonius, *Gaius Caligula,* 21. **Campaign in Germania:** Suetonius, *Gaius Caligula,* 43, and *Galba,* 6.2–3. **Agrippa and Antiochus enthroned:** Philo, *Against Flaccus,* 25, see also 40; Josephus, *Jewish Antiquities,* 18.237; Suetonius, *Gaius Caligula,* 16.3; Dio, *Roman History,* 59.8.2. **Royal coronations in the year 38:** Dio, *Roman History,* 59.12.2. **The palace of Polycrates and the Isthmus of Corinth:** Suetonius, *Gaius Caligula,* 21. **Quotation from Homer:** Suetonius, *Gaius Caligula,* 22.1.

CHAPTER 3. THE CONFLICTS ESCALATE

The Consulars' Conspiracy

Domitian's remark: Suetonius, *Domitian,* 21. **Chants at the theater:** Dio, *Roman History,* 59.13.7. **Corruption in the management of roads:** Dio, *Roman History,* 59.15.3–5. **Caligula's victims in the Senate:** Dio, *Roman History,* 59.18.4–5, 59.19. **C. Calvisius Sabinus:** *Prosopographia Imperii Romani*[2], C 354; Tacitus, *Histories,* 1.48.2; cf. Plutarch, *Galba,* 12. **Titius Rufus:** *Prosopographia Imperii Romani*[1], T 201. **Junius Priscus:** *Prosopographia Imperii Romani*[2], I 801. **Cn. Domitius Afer:** *Prosopographia Imperii Romani*[2], D 126. **Seneca:** Suetonius, *Gaius Caligula,* 53.2.

The Moment of Truth

Speech in the Senate: Dio, *Roman History,* 59.16.2–7; cf. Suetonius, *Gaius Caligula,* 30.2. **Testamentary bequests to Augustus:** Suetonius, *Augustus,* 101.3; cf. 66.4; Tacitus, *Annals,* 1.8.1. **Bequests**

to **Tiberius:** Dio, *Roman History,* 58.16.2. **Bequests to Caligula made compulsory:** Dio, *Roman History,* 59.15.1 and 6. **Contributions to daughter's education:** Suetonius, *Gaius Caligula,* 42. **Coerced gifts and invitations:** Philo, *The Embassy to Gaius,* 343–44. **Caligula's pleasure over aristocrats' lack of power:** Philo, *The Embassy to Gaius,* 344. **Auction of gladiators:** Dio, *Roman History,* 59.14.1–4. **Incitatus:** Dio, *Roman History,* 59.14.7; Suetonius, *Gaius Caligula,* 55.3. **Marriage to Caesonia:** Suetonius, *Gaius Caligula,* 25.3–4; cf. Dio, *Roman History,* 59.23.7. **Date of the wedding:** Meise, *Julisch-claudische Dynastie,* 106–7; Barrett, *Caligula,* 94–95. **Name for Agrippina's son:** Suetonius, *Nero,* 6.2. **Gaetulicus in the reign of Tiberius:** Tacitus, *Annals,* 6.30.2–4. **Incursions by Germanic tribes:** Suetonius, *Tiberius,* 41.

The Great Conspiracy and the Expedition to the North
Consuls removed from office: Dio, *Roman History,* 59.20.2–3. **New consuls:** Cn. Domitius Afer: *Prosopographia Imperii Romani²,* D 126; A. Didius Gallus: *Prosopographia Imperii Romani²,* D 70. **The African legion:** Dio, *Roman History,* 59.20.7; cf. Tacitus, *Histories,* 4.48. **Departure for Germania:** Suetonius, *Gaius Caligula,* 43. **Suetonius's misunderstanding:** cf. Willrich, "Caligula," 307, note 1; Dio, *Roman History,* 59.21. **Documentation on the presence of Lepidus and Caligula's sisters in the retinue:** Seneca, *Moral Epistles (Ad Lucilium Epistulae Morales),* 1.4.7; Dio, *Roman History,* 59.22.8. **Lack of suspicion against sisters documented by later auction in Gaul of their servants, household goods, and jewelry:** Suetonius, *Gaius Caligula,* 39.1. **Explicit references to the great conspiracy in mid-39:** Suetonius, *Claudius,* 9.1, and *Vespasian,* 2.3, cf. *Gaius Caligula,* 24.3; Dio, *Roman History,* 59.22.5–9, 59.23.1; cf. also Balsdon, *Emperor Gaius,* 66–95; Meise, *Julisch-claudische Dynastie,* 91–122. **Suetonius on the reasons for the**

expedition: *Gaius Caligula*, 43; cf. Dio, *Roman History*, 59.21.1–2, 59.22.1. **The conspiracy is foiled:** Suetonius, *Gaius Caligula*, 24.3; Dio, *Roman History*, 59.22.5–9, 59.23.1. **Acta Fratrum Arvalium:** Smallwood, *Documents*, no. 9, p. 14, ll. 18–21. **Conspirators on trial in Rome:** Dio, *Roman History*, 59.23.8. **Vespasian as a praetor:** Suetonius, *Vespasian*, 2.3. **First delegation from the Senate:** Dio, *Roman History*, 59.23.2 and 5 (Dio locates the event in Gaul); Suetonius, *Claudius*, 9.1. **Incursions by Germanic tribes:** Suetonius, *Tiberius*, 41, cf. *Galba*, 6.3. **Military actions on the upper Rhine:** Suetonius, *Gaius Caligula*, 44.1. **On Galba:** Suetonius, *Galba*, 6.2–3, and *Vespasian*, 2.3. **Acclamations as *imperator:*** Dio, *Roman History*, 59.22.2. **Military farce:** Suetonius, *Gaius Caligula*, 45.1. **Tacitus on the military actions:** *Germania*, 37.5; *Histories*, 4.15.3; *Agricola*, 13.4. **Cassius Dio on wealthy Gauls:** *Roman History*, 59.22.3. **Auctions in Gaul:** Suetonius, *Gaius Caligula*, 39; Dio, *Roman History*, 59.21.5–6. **Wealthy Gaul at the emperor's table:** Suetonius, *Gaius Caligula*, 39.2. **Theatrical performances in Gaul:** Dio, *Roman History*, 59.22.1. **Oratorical competition:** Suetonius, *Gaius Caligula*, 20. **Town of Vienna:** Cf. *Inscriptiones Latinae Selectae* 212, col. 2, ll. 15–17. **Events in Rome at the beginning of the year 40:** Dio, *Roman History*, 59.24; Suetonius, *Gaius Caligula*, 17.1. **Prince Adminius:** Suetonius, *Gaius Caligula*, 44.2. **Events at the English Channel:** Suetonius, *Gaius Caligula*, 46; Dio, *Roman History*, 59.25.1–3 (Xiphilinus). **Interpretation of the events:** Balsdon, *Emperor Gaius*, 88–95; more recently Barrett, *Caligula*, 125–39. **Mutiny in the year 43:** Dio, *Roman History*, 60.19.1–3. **Legions punished:** Suetonius, *Gaius Caligula*, 48. **On the situation in Britain:** Barrett, *Caligula*, 127–29. **Tacitus on the military campaigns:** *Germania*, 37.5; *Histories*, 4.15.3; *Agricola*, 13.2. **Triumph and honors prohibited:** Cf. Suetonius, *Gaius Caligula*, 48.2, 49.2.

Reshaping the Emperor's Role

Powerful freedmen under Augustus: Juvenal 1.109, 14.305–8; Suetonius, *Augustus*, 67.1; Dio, *Roman History*, 54.21.3–8. **Under Tiberius:** Josephus, *Jewish Antiquities*, 18.167; Tacitus, *Annals*, 6.38.2. **Caligula's aristocratic retinue in public:** Josephus, *Jewish Antiquities*, 19.102. **Nymphidia:** Plutarch, *Galba*, 9. **Callistus and Domitius Afer:** Dio, *Roman History*, 59.19.6, 59.20.1. **Callistus's position:** Josephus, *Jewish Antiquities*, 19.64–65; cf. Dio, *Roman History*, 59.25.7–8 (Zonaras). **Helicon:** Philo, *The Embassy to Gaius*, 166–83, 203, 205. **Role of Caesonia and the Praetorian prefects:** Suetonius, *Gaius Caligula*, 25.3 f.; Dio, *Roman History*, 59.25.7 (Zonaras and the *Excerpta Vaticana*); Persius 6.43–47. **Imperial procurators, officers of the Praetorian Guard:** Suetonius, *Gaius Caligula*, 47; Josephus, *Jewish Antiquities*, 19.28–29; Suetonius, *Gaius Caligula*, 40.

Triumphantly Crossing the Sea

Presence near Rome in May 40: *Acta Fratrum Arvalium:* Smallwood, *Documents*, no. 10, p. 14, l. 15. **Delegation from the Senate:** Philo, *The Embassy to Gaius*, 181. **Journey to Campania:** Philo, *The Embassy to Gaius*, 185. **Bridge of ships from Puteoli:** Seneca, *On the Shortness of Life* (*De Brevitate Vitae*), 18.5; Josephus, *Jewish Antiquities*, 19.5–6.; Suetonius, *Gaius Caligula*, 19.32.1 (and, on Alexander's breastplate, 52); Dio, *Roman History*, 59.17. (Dating according to the indications given by Seneca and Josephus; Cassius Dio places the event in the year 39 without providing a context.)

CHAPTER 4. FIVE MONTHS OF MONARCHY

Subjugating the Aristocracy

Entrance into Rome: Suetonius, *Gaius Caligula,* 49.2. **Instances of torture under Tiberius:** Suetonius, *Tiberius,* 58; Dio, *Roman History,* 57.19.2. **Plans to eliminate the entire Senate:** Seneca, *On Anger (De Ira)*, 3.19.2; Suetonius, *Gaius Caligula,* 49.2; cf. Dio, *Roman History,* 59.25.5. **Regular executions:** Seneca, *On Anger (De Ira)*, 3.19.1; Suetonius, *Gaius Caligula,* 32.1; cf. 27.3. **Julius Canus:** Seneca, *On Tranquility of Mind (De Tranquillitate Animi)*, 14.4–10; Boethius, *Consolation of Philosophy (Consolatio Philosophiae)*, 1.4.90–94; cf. Plutarch, frg. 211. **Ten-day interval between sentencing and execution in trials for** *maiestas:* Tacitus, *Annals,* 3.51.2. **Julius Graecinus** (*Prosopographia Imperii Romani*[2], I 344): Seneca, *On Favors (De Beneficiis)*, 2.21.5; cf. Seneca, *Moral Epistles (Ad Lucilium Epistulae Morales)*, 29.6; Tacitus, *Agricola,* 4.1. **Agricola's birth** (*Prosopographia Imperii Romani*[2], I 126): Tacitus, *Agricola,* 44.1. **Pomponius and Quintilia:** Josephus, *Jewish Antiquities,* 19.32–36 (Pompedius); Suetonius, *Gaius Caligula,* 16.4 (without mention of the name); Dio, *Roman History,* 59.26.4 (Pomponius). **Sextus Papinius** (*Prosopographia Imperii Romani*[2], P 101), **Betilienus Bassus** (*Prosopographia Imperii Romani*[2], B 114): Seneca, *On Anger (De Ira)*, 3.18.3–19.5; Dio, *Roman History,* 59.25.5b–7. **C. Anicius Cerialis** (*Prosopographia Imperii Romani*[2], A 594): Tacitus, *Annals,* 15.74.3, 16.17.5. **Protogenes in the Senate:** Suetonius, *Gaius Caligula,* 28; Dio, *Roman History,* 59.26.1–2. **The emperor's guard in the Senate:** Suetonius, *Augustus,* 35.1 (Augustus); Dio, *Roman History,* 58.17.3–4. (Tiberius). **Testimony by slaves against their masters:** Josephus, *Jewish Antiquities,* 19.12–14; **under Tiberius:** Dio, *Roman History,* 57.19.2; **under Claudius:** Dio, *Roman History,* 60.15.5.

Claudius on trial: Josephus, *Jewish Antiquities,* 19.12–14; Suetonius, *Claudius,* 9.1. **Aristocratic hostages on the Palatine Hill:**
Suetonius, *Gaius Caligula,* 41.1; Dio, *Roman History,* 59.28.9. **Living
in Augustus's palace:** Dio, *Roman History,* 53.27.5; **in Galba's
palace:** Suetonius, *Galba,* 14.2. **Aristocrats' criticism of Seneca:** Tacitus, *Annals,* 13.42; Dio, *Roman History,* 61.10.1–3.

Dishonoring the Aristocracy

Reserved seating at the theater abolished: Josephus, *Jewish
Antiquities,* 19.86; Suetonius, *Gaius Caligula,* 26.4. **Claudius in the
Senate:** Suetonius, *Claudius,* 9.2. **Dishonoring the noble families:** Suetonius, *Gaius Caligula,* 34.1, 35.1. **Pompeius Magnus**
(*Prosopographia Imperii Romani*[2], P 630): *Inscriptiones Latinae Selectae*
9339; Syme, *Roman Revolution,* 468. **Pompeius's end:** Seneca, *Apocolocyntosis,* 11.2; Suetonius, *Claudius,* 29.1–2; Dio, *Roman History,*
61(60).29.6a. **Flattery continues:** Philo, *The Embassy to Gaius,* 116.
Senators at banquets: Suetonius, *Gaius Caligula,* 26.2. **Submissiveness of aristocrats under Augustus and Tiberius:** Tacitus, *Annals,* 1.2.1, 1.7.1, 1.74.2. **Kissing Caligula's foot:** Dio, *Roman
History,* 59.27.1; Seneca, *On Favors* (*De Beneficiis*), 2.12.1–2 (Pompeius
Poenus). **Kissing actors:** Suetonius, *Gaius Caligula,* 55.1. **Gratitude
for a kiss from the emperor mentioned in the Senate:** Dio,
Roman History, 59.27.1. **Caligula's rhetorical abilities:** Josephus,
Jewish Antiquities, 19.208; Tacitus, *Annals,* 13.3.2; Suetonius, *Gaius
Caligula,* 53.1.

The Emperor as "God"

L. Vitellius: Dio, *Roman History,* 59.27.5. **Dating of his recall
from Syria:** Malalas 10.244 (with confusion about the name); cf.
Josephus, *Jewish Antiquities,* 18.261, and Dio, *Roman History,* as

above. **Senate decree to build a temple to Caligula:** Dio, *Roman History*, 59.28.2; **priesthood for his cult:** Dio, *Roman History*, 59.28.5. **Divine honors for Caesar:** Dio, *Roman History*, 44.6.4. **The *sacrae occupationes* of Tiberius:** Suetonius, *Tiberius*, 27. **Offerings to images of Tiberius and Sejanus:** Dio, *Roman History*, 58.4.4. **A senator prostrates himself:** Tacitus, *Annals*, 1.13.6. **Octavian's "banquet of the twelve gods":** Suetonius, *Augustus*, 70. **Antonius:** Plutarch, *Antonius*, 4.1–2, 24.3, 26.3, 60.2–3. **Augustus's refusal of divine honors:** Suetonius, *Augustus*, 52; cf. Dio, *Roman History*, 51.20.6–7. **Tiberius's rejection of honors and criticism by the Senate:** Tacitus, *Annals*, 4.37–38. **Cult for Tiberius, Livia, and the Senate:** Tacitus, *Annals*, 4.15.3; cf. 4.37–38. **Divinity of the Senate:** Talbert, *Senate*, 96–97. **Caligula's appearances costumed as a god:** Philo, *The Embassy to Gaius*, 78–80, 93–97; Suetonius, *Gaius Caligula*, 52; Dio, *Roman History*, 59.26.10; cf. 59.26.5–7. **On "religious policy":** Willrich, "Caligula," 107–16. **Suetonius on the emperor's clothing:** *Gaius Caligula*, 52. **Epigraphic and numismatic evidence:** Barrett, *Caligula*, 148–49. **"Conversation" with the moon goddess:** Dio, *Roman History*, 59.27.6. **Apelles:** Suetonius, *Gaius Caligula*, 33. **Fee charged to enter the college of the emperor's priests:** Dio, *Roman History*, 59.28.5. **Claudius's prohibition of veneration as a god:** Dio, *Roman History*, 60.5.4. **Scribonius Largus:** *Compositiones* (*praefatio*), 60, 163. **Temple for Nero:** Tacitus, *Annals*, 15.74.3. **Seneca on Claudius's "divine hand":** Seneca, *On Consolation* (*Ad Polybium de Consolatione*), 13.2; cf. Tacitus, *Annals*, 13.42; Dio, *Roman History*, 60.8.5. **Pliny the Elder:** Pliny, *Natural History, praef.* 11. **Philo on Caligula's deification:** *The Embassy to Gaius*, 76 (the emperor's *paraplēxia*). Josephus, *Jewish Antiquities*, 18.256, 19.4 and 11. **Cult of the emperor in Judaea:** cf. Barrett, *Caligula*, 182–91. **Intervention by Agrippa:** Josephus, *Jewish Antiquities*, 18.289–301;

Philo, *The Embassy to Gaius*, 276–329. **Jewish delegation's first audience:** Philo, *The Embassy to Gaius*, 180–83; **second audience:** Philo, *The Embassy to Gaius*, 349–72. **Josephus's descriptions of Caligula before his murder:** *Jewish Antiquities*, 19.87–104. **Suetonius on the deification of Caligula:** *Gaius Caligula*, 22.2–4; cf. 33, 52. **Threat to Jupiter:** Seneca, *On Anger (De Ira)*, 1.20.8–9. **The shoemaker who laughed:** Dio, *Roman History*, 59.26.8–9.

Stability of Rule

For the Praetorian Guard, Germanic bodyguards, and the people of Rome, compare the reports on the reaction to Caligula's assassination: Dio, *Roman History*, 59.30.2, 59.30.1b; Josephus, *Jewish Antiquities*, 19.115, 19.121–22, 19.158–59. **On conflicts with the plebs:** Josephus, *Jewish Antiquities*, 19.24–26; Suetonius, *Gaius Caligula*, 26.5. **L. Vitellius:** *Prosopographia Imperii Romani*[1], V 500; Dio, *Roman History*, 59.27.5–6. **A. Vitellius:** *Prosopographia Imperii Romani*[1], V 499; Suetonius, *Vitellius*, 4, 17.2. **Q. Pomponius Secundus:** *Prosopographia Imperii Romani*[2], P 757; Dio, *Roman History*, 59.29.5. **Cn. Sentius Saturninus:** *Prosopographia Imperii Romani*[1], S 296; Josephus, *Jewish Antiquities*, 19.185. **C. Sallustius Crispus Passienus:** *Prosopographia Imperii Romani*[2], P 146; Suetonius, *Vita Passieni Crispi*. **Valerius Asiaticus:** *Prosopographia Imperii Romani*[1], V 25; Seneca, *On the Firmness of the Wise Man (De Constantia Sapientis)*, 18.2. **Marcus Vinicius:** *Prosopographia Imperii Romani*[1], V 445; Josephus, *Jewish Antiquities*, 19.102. **Annius Vinicianus:** *Prosopographia Imperii Romani*[2], A 701; Josephus, *Jewish Antiquities*, 19.96–98. **Paullus Arruntius:** *Prosopographia Imperii Romani*[2], A 1135; Josephus, *Jewish Antiquities*, 19.102. **On mutual mistrust:** Josephus, *Jewish Antiquities*, 19.51–52. **On Caligula's inner circle:** Dio, *Roman History*, 59.25.7.

Alexandria an Alternative?

On Caligula's plans regarding Alexandria: Philo, *The Embassy to Gaius*, 173, 250, 338; Josephus, *Jewish Antiquities*, 19.81; Suetonius, *Gaius Caligula*, 49.2; cf. 8.5. **On Julius Caesar:** Suetonius, *Julius Caesar*, 79.3. **Marcus Antonius:** Dio, *Roman History*, 50.4.1. **Nero:** Plutarch, *Galba*, 2.1; Dio, *Roman History*, 63.27.2. **On Caligula's conflict with members of his inner circle:** Cassius Dio's quotation, *Roman History* 59.25.8, is a combination of excerpts from Zonaras and the *Excerpta Vaticana*. **Date of planned departure for Alexandria:** Josephus, *Jewish Antiquities*, 19.81; cf. Suetonius, *Gaius Caligula*, 58.1.

CHAPTER 5. MURDER ON THE PALATINE

On secret treachery: Tacitus, *Histories*, 3.68.1. **Core members of the conspiracy:** Josephus, *Jewish Antiquities*, 19.46–48; Suetonius, *Gaius Caligula*, 56.1, 58.2; Dio, *Roman History*, 59.29.1, 59.29.5–6. **Aemilius Regulus, Annius Vinicianus:** Josephus, *Jewish Antiquities*, 19.17–18. **Valerius Asiaticus:** Tacitus, *Annals*, 11.1.2; cf. Josephus, *Jewish Antiquities*, 19.159; Dio, *Roman History*, 59.30.2. **On the emperor's retinue shortly before the assassination:** Josephus, *Jewish Antiquities*, 19.101–2. **Callistus and Claudius:** Josephus, *Jewish Antiquities*, 19.64–69. **The new Praetorian prefect Rufrius Pollio** (*Prosopographia Imperii Romani*[2], R 173): Josephus, *Jewish Antiquities*, 19.267. **The death of the assassins:** Josephus, *Jewish Antiquities*, 19.268–73; Suetonius, *Claudius*, 11.1; Dio, *Roman History*, 60.3.4–5. **The execution of Protogenes and Helicon:** Dio, *Roman History*, 60.4.5; Philo, *The Embassy to Gaius*, 206. **Consultation about the new empress in the year 48:** Tacitus,

Annals, 12.1–2. **On the assassination itself:** Suetonius, *Gaius Caligula*, 56.2, 58; Dio, *Roman History*, 59.29.6–7; Josephus, *Jewish Antiquities*, 19.99–114; Seneca, *On the Firmness of the Wise Man* (*De Constantia Sapientis*), 18.3. **The deaths of Caesonia and Drusilla:** Josephus, *Jewish Antiquities*, 19.198–200 (where their deaths are not shown as immediately following the assassination); Suetonius, *Gaius Caligula*, 59; Dio, *Roman History*, 59.29.7. **On the situation in the theater after the murder:** Josephus, *Jewish Antiquities*, 19.127–57; Dio, *Roman History*, 59.30.1b. **On the session in the Senate:** Josephus, *Jewish Antiquities*, 19.166–89, 19.248–62; Suetonius, *Gaius Caligula*, 60, and *Claudius*, 10.3, 11.1; Dio, *Roman History*, 59.30.3, 60.1–2. **Aspirants to the throne:** Josephus, *Jewish Antiquities*, 19.251–52; Dio, *Roman History*, 60.15.1. **The people in the Forum:** Josephus, *Jewish Antiquities*, 19.158–59. **Claudius's elevation to the throne:** Josephus, *Jewish Antiquities*, 19.162–65, 19.212–26, 19.247; Suetonius, *Claudius*, 10; Dio, *Roman History*, 60.1.3–3a. **Caligula's burial:** Josephus, *Jewish Antiquities*, 19.237; Suetonius, *Gaius Caligula*, 59.

CONCLUSION: INVENTING
THE MAD EMPEROR

On Caligula's "madness": Seneca, *On Anger* (*De Ira*), 1.20.9, 3.21.5, 3.19.3; Philo, *The Embassy to Gaius*, 76, 93; Pliny, *Natural History*, 36.113; Josephus, *Jewish Antiquities*, 18.277, 19.1, 19.4–5, 19.11, 19.193. **Positive assessments:** Philo, *The Embassy to Gaius*, 263; Josephus, *Jewish Antiquities*, 19.208. **Tacitus on Caligula:** *Agricola*, 13.2; *Annals*, 6.20.1, 6.45.3, 11.3.2, 15.72.2; *Histories*, 4.42.5, 4.48.1. **The "madness" of other emperors:** Dio, *Roman History*, 59.1.2; Josephus, *Jewish Antiquities*, 19.259; Tacitus, *Annals*, 6.46.1; Dio, *Roman History*, 63.27.2. **Suetonius on Caligula's mental illness:** *Gaius Caligula*, 50.2–3, 51.1; cf. Dio, *Roman History*, 59.26.5. **Suetonius's *Life of Gaius Caligula* in the reign of Commodus:** *Scriptores Historiae Augustae: Commodus*,

10.2. **On imperial rule in late antiquity:** Kolb, *Herrscherideologie.*
On measures taken by Claudius: Josephus, *Jewish Antiquities,*
19.246; Suetonius, *Claudius,* 11; Dio, *Roman History,* 60.3.5, 60.4.1
and 5, 60.5.1 and 4, 60.22.3. **The conspiracy of Vinicianus and
Camillus:** Dio, *Roman History,* 60.15–16; Suetonius, *Claudius,* 13.2.
Security measures: Dio, *Roman History,* 60.3.3. **Poisoning of
Claudius:** Tacitus, *Annals,* 12.66–67; Dio, *Roman History,* 61(60).34.
On Seneca: Seneca, *On Consolation (Ad Polybium de Consolatione),*
13.2; cf. *Apocolocyntosis,* passim.

BIBLIOGRAPHY

PRIMARY SOURCES

Celsus. *De Medicina.* Vol. 1. Translated by W. G. Spencer. Cambridge, Mass., 1935.

Dio, Cassius. *Roman History.* Vol. 7. Translated by Earnest Cary. Cambridge, Mass., 1955.

Frontinus, Sextus Julius. *The Aqueducts of Rome.* In *Stratagems and the Aqueducts of Rome,* translated by Charles E. Bennett. Cambridge, Mass., 1950.

Josephus, Flavius. *Jewish Antiquities.* Vol. 9. Translated by Louis H. Feldman. Cambridge, Mass., 1965.

Philo of Alexandria. *The Embassy to Gaius.* In vol. 10 of *Philo: Works,* translated by F. H. Colson. Cambridge, Mass., 1962.

Pliny the Elder. *Natural History.* Vol. 10. Translated by H. Rackham. Cambridge, Mass., 1962.

Scriptores Historiae Augustae. 3 vols. Cambridge, Mass., 1967–68.

Seneca. *Apocolocyntosis.* In *Petronius and Seneca,* Loeb Classical Library 15, translated by W. H. D. Rouse, 370–407. Cambridge, Mass., 1975.

———. *De Beneficiis.* In *Moral Essays,* vol. 3, translated by John W. Basore. Cambridge, Mass., 1989.

———. *De Brevitate Vitae.* In *Moral Essays,* vol. 2, translated by John W. Basore, 286–355. Cambridge, Mass., 1932.

————. *De Consolatione ad Helviam.* In *Moral Essays,* vol. 2, translated by John W. Basore, 416–89. Cambridge, Mass., 1932.

————. *De Consolatione ad Polybium.* In *Moral Essays,* vol. 2, translated by John W. Basore, 356–415. Cambridge, Mass., 1932.

————. *De Constantia.* In *Moral Essays,* vol. 1, translated by John W. Basore, 48–105. Cambridge, Mass., 1951.

————. *De Ira.* In *Moral Essays,* vol. 1, translated by John W. Basore. Cambridge, Mass., 1951.

————. *De Tranquillitate Animi.* In *Moral Essays,* vol. 2, translated by John W. Basore, 202–85. Cambridge, Mass., 1932.

————. *Epistulae Morales.* 3 vols. Translated by Richard M. Gummere. Cambridge, Mass., 1917–25.

Suetonius. *Lives of the Caesars.* In *Suetonius.* 2 vols. Translated by J.C. Rolfe. Cambridge, Mass., 1997–98.

————. *Vita Passieni Crispi.* In *Suetonius,* vol. 2, translated by J.C. Rolfe, 482–83. Cambridge, Mass., 1997–98.

Tacitus. *Agricola.* In *Tacitus,* vol. 1, translated by John Jackson. Cambridge, Mass., 1980.

————. *Annals.* In *Tacitus,* vols. 3–5, translated by John Jackson. Cambridge, Mass., 1970–81.

————. *Germania.* In *Tacitus,* vol. 1, translated by John Jackson. Cambridge, Mass., 1980.

————. *The Histories.* In *Tacitus,* vols. 2 and 3, translated by John Jackson. Cambridge, Mass., 1970–81.

SECONDARY SOURCES

Auguet, Roland. *Caligula; ou, Le pouvoir à vingt ans.* Paris, 1984.

Balsdon, John P.V.D. *The Emperor Gaius (Caligula).* Oxford, 1934 [Reprint 1964].

Barrett, Anthony A. *Agrippina: Mother of Nero.* London, 1990.

————. *Caligula: The Corruption of Power.* London, 1989.

Boschung, Dietrich. *Die Bildnisse des Caligula.* Berlin, 1989.

Champlin, Edward. *Nero.* Cambridge, Mass., and London, 2003.

Ferrill, Arthur. *Caligula: Emperor of Rome.* London, 1991.

Flashar, Hellmut. *Melancholie und Melancholiker in den medizinischen Theorien der Antike.* Berlin, 1966.

Garnsey, Peter, and Richard P. Saller. *The Roman Empire: Economy, Society and Culture.* London, 1987.

Gelzer, Matthias. "Iulius 133 [Caligula]." In *Paulys Realencyclopädie der classischen Altertumswissenschaft,* vol. 10.1, 381–423. Stuttgart, 1918.

Hopkins, Keith, and Graham P. Burton. "Ambition and Withdrawal: The Senatorial Aristocracy under the Emperors." In Keith Hopkins, *Death and Renewal: Sociological Studies in Roman History,* vol. 2, 120–200. Cambridge, 1983.

Kienast, Dietmar. *Römische Kaisertabelle: Grundzüge einer römischen Kaiserchronologie.* 2nd ed. Darmstadt, 1996.

Kolb, Frank. *Herrscherideologie in der Spätantike.* Berlin, 2001.

Lendon, John E. *Empire of Honour: The Art of Government in the Roman World.* Oxford, 1997.

Levick, Barbara. *Claudius.* London, 1990.

———. *Tiberius the Politician.* London, 1976.

Meier, Christian. "C. Caesar Divi filius and the Formation of the Alternative in Rome." In *Between Republic and Empire: Interpretations of Augustus and His Principate,* edited by Kurt A. Raaflaub and Mark Toher, 54–70. Berkeley and Los Angeles, 1990.

Meise, Eckhard. *Untersuchungen zur Geschichte der julisch-claudischen Dynastie.* Munich, 1969.

Midelfort, H. C. Erik. *Mad Princes of Renaissance Germany.* Charlottesville and London, 1994.

Millar, Fergus. *The Emperor in the Roman World (31 B.C.–A.D. 337).* 2nd ed. London, 1992.

Mommsen, Theodor. *Römisches Staatsrecht.* 3 vols. in 5. 3rd ed. Leipzig, 1887.

Nony, Daniel. *Caligula.* Paris, 1986.

Quidde, Ludwig. "Caligula: Eine Studie über römischen Cäsarenwahnsinn" [1894]. In *Ludwig Quidde, Caligula: Schriften über Militarismus und Pazifismus,* edited by Hans-Ulrich Wehler, 61–80. Frankfurt am Main, 1977.

Rilinger, Rolf. "Domus und res publica: Die politisch-soziale Bedeutung des aristokratischen 'Hauses' in der späten römischen Republik." In *Ordo und dignitas: Beiträge zur römischen Verfassungs- und Sozialgeschichte,* 105–22. Stuttgart, 2007.

Roller, Matthew B. *Constructing Autocracy: Aristocrats and Emperors in Julio-Claudian Rome.* Princeton and Oxford, 2001.

Sachs, Hanns. *Bubi Caligula.* 2nd ed. Vienna, 1932.

Saller, Richard P. *Personal Patronage under the Early Empire.* Cambridge, 1982.

Siegel, Rudolph E. *Galen on Psychology, Psychopathology, and Function and Diseases of the Nervous System: An Analysis of His Doctrines, Observations and Experiments.* Basel, 1973.

Smallwood, E. Mary. *Documents Illustrating the Principates of Gaius, Claudius and Nero.* Cambridge, 1967.

Syme, Ronald. *The Roman Revolution.* Oxford, 1939.

Talbert, Richard J. A. *The Senate of Imperial Rome.* Princeton, 1984.

Timpe, Dieter. "Römische Geschichte bei Flavius Josephus." *Historia* 9 (1960): 474–502.

Veyne, Paul. *Le pain et le cirque: Sociologie historique d'un pluralisme politique.* Paris, 1976.

Wilkinson, Sam. *Caligula.* London and New York, 2005.

Willrich, Hugo. "Caligula." *Klio* 3 (1903): 85–118, 288–317, 397–470.

Winterling, Aloys. *Aula Caesaris: Studien zur Institutionalisierung des römischen Kaiserhofes in der Zeit von Augustus bis Commodus (31 v. Chr.–192 n. Chr.).* Munich, 1999.

———. "Cäsarenwahnsinn im Alten Rom." In *Jahrbuch des Historischen Kollegs 2007,* 115–39. Munich, 2008.

———. *Politics and Society in Imperial Rome.* Oxford, 2009.

Wolters, Reinhard. "Die Organisation der Münzprägung in julisch-claudischer Zeit." *Numismatische Zeitschrift* 106/107 (1999): 75–90.

Yavetz, Zvi. "Caligula, Imperial Madness and Modern Historiography." *Klio* 78 (1996): 105–29.

INDEX

In this index, "f" refers to a separate mention on the next page, "ff" to separate mentions on the next two pages, and "passim" to separate mentions on pages in close but not necessarily consecutive sequence. Page numbers in italics refer to illustrations.

Well-known Roman figures (as, for example, emperors and the members of their families) are listed in this index according to their customary names as used in the text proper; all others are listed according to their gentilicians.

Praetorian prefects, 27, 30, 64, 71,
121ff, 165, 171, 174ff, 178. *See also*
Macro; Sejanus
princeps, 15, 23, 52, 59f, 73, 77, 120,
149f, 164
Principate, 11, 15, 18, 58, 61, 69, 99,
149f. *See also* emperorship;
honors: imperial renunciation
of; *princeps*
procurators, 123, 136, 170
Propertius, 149
proskynēsis and prostration, 116, 146,
147–48, 149, 155, 158, 192. *See also*
ceremonies
Protogenes, 122, 137, 165–75 passim
Ptolemy (king of Mauretania), 125
Puteoli, 127f, 130f, 152

Quidde, Ludwig, 2, 191
Quintilia, 135, 146, 177

rank, social, 13, 29, 74f, 81, 103f, 121,
124–26, 130, 143, 146f, 163, 167. *See
also* society
rationes imperii, 67
religion, 148, 156. *See also* deification; divine veneration;
emperor cult
Republic, Roman, 11ff, 15, 24, 68ff,
72f, 78, 84f, 124f, 143, 149f, 152, 167,
183, 185. *See also* paradox: of
republic vs. monarchy
Rhegium, 85
Rhodes, 21
Rhoemetalces, 88
rivalries, 18, 22, 32, 35, 57, 61f, 64, 66,
73, 88–89; among aristocracy, 18,
25, 26–28, 168; of emperor vs.
aristocracy, 28, 85, 145, 166
road networks, Roman, 94
Romulus, 66
Rufrius Pollio, 175

Saepta, 69
C. Sallustius Crispus, 164, 193
salutatio, 14, 25f, 29, 73–74, 75f, 101,
140, 152, 156
Samos, 88
Q. Sanquinius Maximus, 90
Scribonius Largus, 155
Scribonius Proculus, 137–38, 141
Sejanus, 26–40 passim, 48, 50, 56,
97, 139, 149
Seleucus, 43
Senate, 5, 12, 23–24, 25f, 44, 65,
69–70, 96–104 passim, 116–31
passim, 137–38, 143, 150–51,
182–86. *See also homines novi;
nobilitas;* nobility; rank, social;
senatorial order
senatorial order, 3–4, 28, 68, 78,
84–85, 96–97, 102, 120, 122, 134,
137, 150, 163, 165f. *See also homines
novi; nobilitas*
Seneca, 1, 3, 81f, 86, 93, 96, 129–46
passim, 155–56, 159–60, 181,
188–89, 193–94
Cn. Sentius Saturninus, 164,
183–84, 188
Sextius Paconianus, 38
sexuality, 38, 47, 48–49, 79, 139. *See
also* incest
ships, 76, 127ff
shrines and temples: in Syracuse,
86; of Augustus, 58, 183; of
Caligula, 148, 151, 156f, 183; of
Castor and Pollux, 151; of
Drusilla, 82; of Julius Caesar,
149; of Mars Ultor, 110; of *Roma et
Augustus*, 150; of Solomon
(Jewish, in Jerusalem), 156f; of
the Arval Brethren, 126; of
Tiberius, Livia, and the Senate,
150, 183; of Venus, 82; on the
Capitol, 116; to Nero, 136, 155

Text: 10.75/15 Janson MT Pro
Display: Janson MT Pro
Compositor: Binghamton Valley Composition, LLC
Printer and binder: Maple-Vail Manufacturing Group